The Family Therapy Collections

James C. Hansen, Series Editor

Lucille L. Andreozzi, Volume Editor

INTEGRATING
RESEARCH
AND
CLINICAL
PRACTICE

CALIFORNIA SCHOOL OF PROFESSIONAL PSYCHOLOGY LOS ANGELES

with
Ronald F. Levant,
Consulting Editor

AN ASPEN PUBLICATION®
Aspen Systems Corporation
Rockville, Maryland
Royal Tunbridge Wells
1985

Library of Congress Cataloging-in-Publication Data
Main entry under title:

Integrating research and clinical practice.

(The Family therapy collections, ISSN: 0735-9152;15)
"An Aspen publication."
Includes bibliographies and index.

1. Family psychotherapy. 2. Family psychotherapy—Research.
I. Andreozzi, Lucille L. II. Levant, Ronald F. III. Series. [DNLM: 1. Family Therapy.
2. Research. W1 FA454N v.15 / WM 430.5.F2 I603]
RC488.5.I5   1985   616.89'156   85-15699
ISBN: 0-89443-615-5

Editorial Services: Ruth Bloom

The Family Therapy Collections series is indexed in
Psychological Abstracts and the PsycINFO database

Library of Congress Catalog Card Number: 85-15699
ISBN: 0-89443-615-5
ISSN: 0735-9152

Printed in the United States of America

1 2 3 4 5

Table
of
Contents

Board of Editors

Series Preface

FAMILY THERAPY COLLEC-tions is a quarterly publication in which topics of current and specific interest to family therapists are presented. Each volume serves as a source of information for practicing therapists by translating theory and research into practical applications. Authored by practicing professionals, the articles in each volume provide in-depth coverage of a single aspect of family therapy.

This volume focuses on the relationship between research and clinical practice. Many clinicians believe that research is irrelevant to their practice, that they have no time to do research, or that their participation in research studies would divert them from their major purposes as family therapists. Several articles in this volume illustrate that research and practice can be integrated, however. Research need not be defined in terms of statistics and published articles. It also involves the thought processes and data analyses that the clinician uses to make decisions about treatment.

It is clear that, in order to make research findings more broadly applicable, the set of conventions used in designing family therapy research must differ from that used in individual therapy. Often, however, researchers strive for rigorous methods to establish a science, while practitioners want relevant information to use in working with families. There is a need for rigor in research methods, of course, but reports can also describe techniques and approaches that practitioners can apply. Because the authors in this volume are both practitioners and researchers, they are well qualified to discuss the issues involved in integrating research and therapy, as well as to provide examples of applications.

This volume grew out of a conference on the assessment of family therapy at the 1983 Annual Meeting of the National Council on Family Relations. Dr. Ronald F. Levant, Clinical Associate Professor at Boston University, developed the program which was intended to examine the issues of family therapy and family therapy outcome research. New administrative responsibilities prohibited Dr. Levant from editing the volume and Dr. Lucille L. Andreozzi assumed the editorial responsibility with consultation from Dr. Levant.

The editor of this volume, Lucille L. Andreozzi, is a research associate at the Family Center in Somerville, Massachusetts. She is involved in the development of family therapy research strategies that are integrated with family therapy practice in a way that positively influences therapy outcomes. In Rhode Island, she coordinated a 5-year state-wide study of early intervention programs for diverse populations of families with specific common needs or concerns (e.g., families at risk for child abuse, families with handicapped children, and economically disadvantaged families). Dr. Andreozzi also designed and con-

ducted a 3-year family therapy outcome study involving families in which the children were having problems. Clearly, her experience both as a researcher and therapist provide Dr. Andreozzi with the perspective to edit this volume.

James C. Hansen
Series Editor

Preface

THE FIELD OF FAMILY therapy has generated a vast array of theoretical orientations, methods, and techniques to treat marital and family distress. Research efforts have increased in direct response to the proliferation of therapy methods and techniques, as well as to the awareness that full descriptions of the ways in which such methods and techniques actually work are required in order to understand them completely. These research efforts, directed largely toward the assessment of therapy and explication of the therapy process, have yielded considerable data on the effects and effectiveness of marital and family therapy—an issue of critical importance to both researchers and practitioners. The impact of research (its results, the questions posed, the strategies used) and the impact of therapy (events in the therapy hour) are, in many respects, interdependent and reflect a relationship of mutual influence.

The purpose of this volume is to highlight the relevance and utility of family therapy research and research findings for the practice of family therapy. This volume is an effort to bridge the gap between the two worlds of practice and research, to dissipate some of the professional division, and to dissolve some of the pragmatic "barriers" that have often stood in the way of a more mutually beneficial relationship between the practice of therapy and the practice of research.

The contributors to this volume represent a wide range of viewpoints and offer a variety of recommendations, practical suggestions, and applications that demonstrate the critical importance of research to practice. While each author provides a decidedly individual treatment and interpretation of the status of research and its implications for effective therapy, they agree that research and therapy are intimately allied and closely related companion activities. Their practical discussions on the state of the art and science of family therapy research will help clinicians to enhance their research skills, as well as to incorporate the knowledge derived from research in their routine practice.

In "Why Outcome Research Fails the Family Therapist," Andreozzi addresses therapists' perceptions that traditional outcome research often functions at cross purposes with the application of therapy methods and attempts to highlight ways in which clinicians routinely perform researcher-like activities. Wamboldt, Wamboldt, and Gurman, in "Marital and Family Therapy Research: The Meaning for the Clinician," summarize and describe important themes gleaned from prior review efforts and more recent studies on marital and family therapy and discuss the implications of these findings for family therapy practice. Their overview of salient themes identified in existing outcome research provides a frame of reference for the status of empirical findings derived from current research.

Steier presents a discussion of the dilemmas encountered in family therapy assessment and the process of outcome research in "New Paradigms for the Evaluation of Family Therapy Research." He describes these dilemmas as mismatches in the paradigmatic bases of therapy practice and therapy research programs that complicate clinical and research interpretations of outcome, and he recommends a cybernetic approach to family therapy efficacy research. Kantor and Andreozzi, in "The Cybernetics of Family Therapy and Family Therapy Research," describe the application of cybernetic principles to a research project currently under way at the Family Center in Somerville, Massachusetts. They not only illustrate the operation of cybernetic principles in the therapy-research enterprise, but also offer useful questions that therapists can ask about their work and interaction with clients. In " 'Circularity' in the Management of a Case," Kantor uses a case from the ongoing Family Center research project to depict the multifaceted aspects of the therapy process and multiple levels of therapy outcome, as well as to demonstrate that the therapy-process-outcome feedback loop extends far beyond client-therapist-therapy method interaction to include such influences as the research and research instruments.

In "Dyadic Interaction Patterns," Ravich notes the parallel between the shift in focus in family therapy from the individual to relationships and the shift in focus in the neurosciences from the neuron to the synapse. He then describes the clinical uses and applications of game theory for the assessment, diagnosis, and treatment of dyadic interactions and marital therapy. Guerney, in "The Medical versus the Educational Model as a Base for Family Therapy Research," compares and contrasts the uses and assumptions underlying the medical and the educational models, recommending the educational model for both research and therapy.

In "The Conflict between the Ethics of Therapy and Outcome Research in Family Therapy," Jurich and Russell call attention to the often compelling and conflictual choices that must be made when the demands and restraints of research design meet the interests and concerns of clients and the therapists who are entrusted to help them.

Finally, in "Family Therapy Practice and Research: A Dialogue," Keeney and Morris construct a dialogue between therapist and researcher. They compare a cybernetic view of science to other scientific epistemologies and propose new, alternate approaches to clinical research and practice.

Cumulatively, the articles in this volume present a discussion and consolidation of major themes and trends in family therapy research. It is hoped that the concepts, issues, and perspectives offered in this volume will contribute to a climate of greater dialogue and interaction between therapists and researchers.

Lucille L. Andreozzi, Ed.D.
Volume Editor

1

Why Outcome Research Fails the Family Therapist

Lucille L. Andreozzi, Ed.D.
The Family Center
Somerville, Massachusetts

F AMILY THERAPY RESEARCH strategies need to be made more adaptable to clinical methods of practice. The need for objectivity and the linear sequencing of events characteristic of traditional outcome research in family therapy should be reevaluated in light of the clinical questions that currently confront the family therapist. Research strategies should be applied more systemically and should function as tools of information exchange so that researchers can respond to clinicians at more appropriately timed moments in therapy. The overall research enterprise should be integrated into the family therapy process.

Therapists and researchers are kindred spirits; therapy and research reflect parallel, overlapping, even synonymous activities. The dissimilarities between them are more a product of professional conditioning than a sign of fundamental differences in their underlying intentions and functions. In short, family therapy process and outcome are interdependent. To understand and study one is to understand, study, and, at times, make assumptions about the other.

The evaluation of the effectiveness of family therapy should extend beyond the assessment of a given therapeutic method to include the *influence* of all system participants, most notably the therapist, but also such individuals as supervisors, client families, family center staff, and researchers. Just as data elicited on multiple, concurrent family system levels (e.g., identified patient, marital dyad, parental dyad) sometimes reveal different or discrepant views on outcome (Andreozzi, in press), data gathered on multiple family therapy process levels (e.g., therapist, super-

1

visors, referral agencies) often suggest varied perspectives on outcome.

Ideally, family therapists and family therapy researchers should interact. Therefore, clinicians need to view research less as something imposed on practice or as an evaluation process so removed from clinical interaction that the information it yields is neither useful nor, at times, recognizable. They must realize that, in essence, to do effective family therapy is to do family therapy research (Kantor, 1985; Kantor & Andreozzi, 1985).

FAMILY THERAPISTS' VIEW OF RESEARCH

The responses of clinicians to the prospect of research often range from mild enthusiasm and/or disinterest to openly declared skepticism. Not only are therapists sensitized to underlying discrepancies between the researcher's construction of reality (including the language used) and the clinical realities facing the therapist, but also therapists seem fundamentally unconvinced of the immediate and direct benefits of research for practice. Therapists, who have a critical need for information in their provision of services, seem, in their skeptical stance, to be challenging the researchers to provide useful, readily available suggestions that will enhance practice and ultimately promote the well-being of clients.

To many therapists, the word *research* suggests more work with little immediate professional gratification in return. The association instantly evoked by the phrase *outcome research* may be a traditional experiment in which a random sample of families is randomly assigned to research conditions (e.g., to therapy,

wait-lists, or no therapy, or to one of several comparable forms of treatment). Families are pretested on assessment measures. Therapists provide treatment(s). Families are posttested with perhaps an additional follow-up assessment. Researchers code and analyze the data, and the results on outcome are compared to determine the effects of the intervention(s) (Campbell & Stanley, 1963). Such associations may be established first by academic training and professional specialization, and then later reinforced by the way treatment agencies are organized. The implication is unmistakable—research and therapy worlds are kept separate; they represent different activities; research takes place "outside" therapy.

Therapists raise their objections to group design research strategies in three interrelated areas: the theoretical, the practical, and the ethical. On theoretical grounds, therapists are not convinced that group design models are compatible with family therapy as a specific conceptual approach to family distress. It is not uncommon to hear therapists ask, "How can such linear cause-effect statements and measures of change adequately, accurately, or fairly approximate our concepts of circular causality, family systems, and family systems change?"

A therapist who is disenchanted with the analytical distance that must be traveled in order to translate and apply a column of inferential statistics to the clinical realities of families in treatment may argue, "Group comparisons, randomization, and multivariate methods may work well for the study of agricultural crop rotations, but what can they do in the study of complex systems, such as the family, not to mention the family therapist-therapy enterprise?'' Busy therapists who do not have the time or inclination to ponder statistical technology may contend that tables and charts do not adequately reflect the multitude of variables and complex events that occur within any given therapy hour. Those therapists familiar with the array of comprehensive reviews on outcome and process research (e.g., Gurman, 1973; Gurman & Kniskern, 1978a, 1981; Jacobson, 1978; Pinsof, 1981; Todd & Stanton, 1983; Wells, Dilkes & Trivelli, 1972) and the debates on empirical, clinical, and conceptual issues in marital and family therapy (e.g., Gurman & Kniskern, 1978b; Gurman & Knudson, 1978; Gurman, Knudson & Kniskern, 1978; Jacobson & Weiss, 1978) may argue that, except on basic and/or major points, reviewers do not always seem to agree. In addition, a companion literature challenges the validity of empirical findings, the researchers' punctuation of outcome, the meaning of system and symptom, and the view of outcome based almost exclusively on knowledge from experimental research (Allman, 1982; Colapinto, 1979; Dell, 1982; Keeney, 1979, 1982a, 1982b; Keeney & Sprenkle, 1982). Therapists, aware of this literature, believe that the data on outcome raise more questions than they answer.

On a practical level, therapists often feel that research protocols work at cross-purposes with effective clinical practice, that they are cumbersome operations, and that they can interfere with immediate, effective client-therapist interaction. Indeed, therapists convinced of the impracticalities of research protocols find objections on ethical grounds, raising several clinical dilemmas. For example, is the need for randomization in group design research strategies adequate justification for withholding treatment from some families? Do wait-lists and control group strategies provide levels and types of data that are worth the emotional cost they exact from clients? When there is a choice of treatments, which of two or more equally valued therapies should be provided to which families or group of families? Thus, the skepticism of the therapist, acting as a judicious ally and advocate for families, often safeguards the client's rights to responsible, qualified treatment.

THE THERAPY-RESEARCH DILEMMA

Group outcome models represent the most frequently used type of research in marital and family therapy. Confidence in findings derived from these studies depends largely on the satisfactory fulfillment of the model's articulated assumptions and requirements (e.g., homogeneity of population; randomization; replicable, operational treatments; treatment validity; objective measures and controls). Ironically, however, when these models are most successfully applied, they may fail the family therapist on organizational, clinical, and conceptual grounds, further contributing to the perceived paradigmatic mismatch between the conduct of research and therapy on issues such as the timing of information on therapeutic interventions, the way in which outcome is punctuated and therapy methods are applied, the interpretation of outcome, and the way self-referential operations are viewed within the structure of traditional research experiments. The message conveyed to therapists is rigorous research methods constrain or even conflict with practice. Consequently, the close relationship between therapy and research and the link between doing effective therapy and doing effective family therapy research are weakened rather than strengthened as they should be.

Timing of Information Exchange

Usually, the therapist receives information from outcome research only *after* family therapy has ended. While it is productive for the researcher to wait until the results of the family therapy process are in and the data analysis has been completed, therapists would benefit more readily from information on the progress of therapy almost as it is occurring. When therapists must wait to be provided with the data, they must "go back" in time and, perhaps, professional development to incorporate or rework these data, matching the data (e.g., statistical tables) with their recollections. The task is so time-consuming that therapists often feel they get little in return for their mental efforts. Furthermore, trying to relate clinical events and client-therapist interactions retrospectively (via case notes and personal impressions) to family therapy outcome (e.g., group mean scores) can have several counterproductive effects.

First, the process of providing therapists with general data on outcome moves the clinician further away from a close, intimate, and accurate examination of therapy events with an individual family. Second, since recollections tend at times to be clouded and self-selective, and case summaries do not always contain all the interpersonal nuances of therapy relationships, a great deal of

clinically enlightening information on therapy outcome may be lost to the therapist; the therapist may unwittingly overlook, omit, or forget important outcome information.

The timing of outcome data in traditional experimental studies may make it impossible for the therapist to identify patterns underlying case treatments. For example, do therapists change their behavior when they encounter different types of problems (e.g., adolescent drug abuse versus teen-age pregnancy) or when they encounter the same problem type (e.g., child development problems) with males versus females from different types of families (e.g., upper middle class, lower middle class)? With the recognition that therapy is sometimes more effective, sometimes less effective, therapists would undoubtedly benefit from outcome information that sheds light on both positive and negative therapy patterns from the therapist's perspective, client experience, and overall outcome.

Outcome studies convey a strong message to clinicians. The delay in information exchange between therapist and researcher suggests not only that there is a gap between therapy and research, but also that outcome is a single, end-product "event" of therapy. It is just such concepts that often make therapists reluctant participants in research.

Outcome as Therapy Punctuation

Family therapists often disagree with the way that outcome research strategies tend to punctuate the family therapy experience. Outcome studies routinely focus on the differences that can be observed in families after therapy. Whether a therapeutic method is compared to a competitive form of equally effective therapy or whether the general effects of family therapy are compared to the results of no intervention, these studies imply to therapists that outcome is a single event that can be easily measured, documented, and analyzed. This concept of outcome seems, in the end, to offer therapists a composite description of outcome that either fragments the family change they observed in therapy or presents the change as if it were a freeze-frame picture of family progress.

Therapists know that no two families respond in exactly the same way to the same family therapy method, regardless of how faithfully the method is applied. Therapists also know that outcome is not a single moment that can be described, for example, in a set of responses on family therapy outcome questionnaires. Outcome is varied and multidimensional; it includes the tracking of change on multiple, often simultaneous system levels (e.g., family unit, marital unit, parental unit, sibling unit) and encompasses a variety of perspectives (e.g., therapist, family, treatment agency, referring agency).

Therapists also recognize that outcome does not happen at the end of therapy. Family therapy is a continuous, unfolding process in which a series of smaller outcomes build to produce the final outcome that researchers measure and compare. Outcome and process are mutually interdependent. Therapists know, for example, that the final therapy outcome is influenced by all moments of contact with the family, even including the family's first telephone call for help. Research often fails the family therapist because it does not adequately capture either the interaction of process and out-

come or the influence of process events on outcome (Andreozzi, in press).

Interpretation of Outcome

The judgments or interpretations that therapists and researchers bring to the way in which they categorize value-laden family events is ultimately subjective. In placing so much emphasis on "objectivity" and "objective measures of change," however, researchers often sidestep this issue. Aware of the complexities underlying decisions on the success of therapy, therapists may sense the ironies in researchers' claims that their methods and models are objective when, in fact, these methods and models are inevitably subjective.

To complicate matters further, therapists may feel—quite accurately—that group outcome studies do not adequately address differing opinions of outcome among family members and even among treatment agencies. For example, what happens when the husband feels therapy was helpful and the wife does not? If a family is more openly expressing disagreements at the end of therapy, ironically obtaining *lower* post-therapy scores on family communication or family functioning questionnaires, does this mean that the therapy has failed? Or, does it mean that the therapy, in allowing disagreements to surface, has been generally successful? Therapists believe that the interpretation of outcome requires an overall consideration of context and the individual content of a given family case.

Outcome research may disappoint the family therapist in that it, at times, appears not to address these issues (Andreozzi, in press), glossing over such dilemmas. When research focuses primarily on group outcome, whether derived from subjective client self-reports or objective measures of change, it may lose the family therapist who is trained to respond to subtleties and look beyond first global impressions.

Position of the Therapist in the Feedback Loop

Group outcome research, by design, places the therapist outside the family therapy feedback loop. Because researchers believe that therapists are part of the therapy method being "tested," they believe that therapists, like the therapy, must remain independent of the assessment. Thus, in order to ensure objectivity and a valid test of the therapy method in use, the knowledge and feedback that the research tools may be gathering before and during therapy are kept away from the therapist.

The need to keep the therapy and the research separate in the study of family therapy methods and their impact on outcome is primarily a function of the structure of the research model. This is a frustrating and often clinically unproductive situation for the therapist and families in treatment, however. Moreover, it is ironic that, in recognizing the therapist's effects on methods and families and in trying to control these effects in the study, the research actually fails to address this complex relationship. On one level, therapists are acknowledged as critically influential on therapy, client, and outcome; yet, on another level, their influence is ignored.

Treatment of Self-Referential Operations

Just as all families do not respond to family therapy in the same way, a therapist does not respond to all families in the same way. While therapists try, as best they can, to remain aware that they like and/or dislike some families and family members, trying to prevent these personal feelings from interfering in the overall therapy, these relationship factors and ways of intuitively responding and interacting with client families are realities of therapy (Kantor, 1985; Kantor & Andreozzi, 1985). The group design models do not regularly accommodate the study of such self-referential operations, however. With its heavy emphasis on the study and comparison of therapy methods, the group outcome strategy minimizes the personal idiosyncracies in therapists' styles of relating to families. Instead of allowing these "relationship structures" to be studied, corrected, and/or put to good clinical use, research strategies treat these operations as "flaws" in the study. Even though such knowledge of how and when therapists become too personally involved with specific family types would undoubtedly enhance both clinical practice and the development of individual therapists, self-referential operations are removed from the cycle of influence and the feedback loop that is ultimately responsible for both the range of outcomes reported in therapy and the interpretation of each outcome.

Therapists may, therefore, argue that family therapy is not a completely replicable intervention. While methods provide guidelines and some methods involve more clearly specified treatment plans than do others, therapy is a human endeavor. As such, there will be moments when therapists, for the right or wrong reasons, "deviate" from the treatment plans/method. It seems advisable to acknowledge this and to study such "deviations" for what they reveal about family process, therapy outcome, patterns of change, and new problem-solving techniques.

Application of Family Therapy Methods

Outcome studies usually approach a family therapy treatment as if it were a homogeneous activity rather than a complex set of steps or events. In addition, treatment methods are usually reported in the literature as if they were single, specific treatments applied without variation to all families. It is often assumed that the therapy method tested is uniformly and identically applied by all therapists. Yet, when therapists' in-session behaviors are examined in relation to the proposed treatment, it has been noted that not only do therapists vary therapeutic techniques within sessions and across families but also that the therapy method defined is often not the therapy tested. The therapy method actually tested frequently contains techniques associated with other therapy methods. Gurman and Kniskern (1978b) and Pinsof (1981) describe, for example, that in five of the six most well designed comparative studies on behavioral family therapy, therapists also employed techniques associated with other therapy methods (e.g., humanistic, client-centered approaches). Therefore, the therapists were providing a treatment that encompassed features beyond the defined behavioral approach.

Such variations in method application occur during therapy more frequently than researchers may like to admit. Discrepancies between the therapist's professed orientation and in-session application of the therapy method create a dilemma in outcome research because of the ways in which these studies are organized and approached. After all, one underlying assumption of group outcome studies is that the treatment tested is, indeed, the therapy applied. Although such discrepancies cast some confusion on the study's outcome implications from a researcher's standpoint, therapists may profit from a systematic study of these therapy events.

Research frustrates clinicians on one level by providing them with information on the outcome of therapy methods that is difficult to interpret (e.g., which method or components of the method actually contributed to the positive effects of therapy?) and on another level by depriving them of systematic explanations for how or even why discrepancies occur. If family therapy researchers move away from tests of competitive therapy approaches and toward the study of the common elements of effective therapy across methods, therapists may become more willing to commit themselves to the research enterprise.

Emphasis on the Group Effect

To clinicians, research approaches often suggest that all families are alike and display the same or similar responses to all phases and/or subphases of treatment; that the differential effects of therapy can be easily summarized and studied; that therapy outcomes can indeed be accurately or fully described solely on the group level; and finally, that the so-called homogeneous populations of both families and problems do not, in many instances, contain diverse subpopulations. Yet, therapists know that, whether a therapist or therapy method "sees" and "treats" only the initial problem or "sees" the initial problem as masking other equally compelling family problems, the problem for which families originally seek help may not be the problem that troubles them the most. For example, a child's problem can sometimes deflect the parents' attention from more deeply rooted marital problems that lie at the heart of the family's distress.

Although group results (i.e., both the average response and group variability in the application of family therapy) may have statistical significance in some instances, these findings do not always convey the types of changes that occur within families. When individual family cases are studied both as individual patterns of change (i.e., the family in comparison to itself as it progresses over time) and in relation to the overall group effect (i.e., the average family response), however, several trends may appear. Within any given homogeneous population of families who seek help for the same general problem type, for example, some families may improve steadily; others may remain relatively the same; others may show the negative effects of therapy; and still others may report conflicting family member evaluations on the therapy process at the end of therapy, only to report positive family change or a shift toward improvement at follow-up. The patterns of change may be as individualistic and idiosyncratic across outcome measures as are the families themselves. Emphasis on group outcome without equal attention to individual family change may seriously overshadow or even obscure information on the subpatterns of individual family development and change that is critically important to therapists.

INTEGRATION OF FAMILY THERAPY AND FAMILY THERAPY RESEARCH

When the different technologies (methods and techniques) and different languages in which therapists and researchers frame their respective realities are laid aside, therapists and researchers have much in common. Therapists often use researcher-like activities. In formulating a family systems diagnosis, for example, therapists develop working hypotheses on change. Often assessed and sometimes revised, these hypotheses guide the therapists in the uses of their therapy method. When a therapist formulates a family systems diagram (i.e., a representation of the family structure before therapy) and a diagram of desired systems change (i.e., the eventual family structure if therapy is successful), the therapist not only is inferring a therapeutic plan, but also is describing a before-and-after measure of difference.

In addition, when therapists elicit family members' views on the problem, they are essentially researching the problem. Throughout the unfolding course of therapy and the interactions between therapist and client family, therapists are usually exploring changes and the effects of change. As a member of the therapy system who both influences and is influenced by it, the therapist is continually researching the progress and the effects of the therapy on the family. In certain instances, when the therapist obtains new information, the therapist may change strategies.

While the therapist stands often at the center of the family therapy experience and family therapy outcome in relation to client families, other participants also influence the overall family therapy enterprise. A panorama of constituents, including supervisors, center staff, clients, and referring agencies, and the organized ways in which they communicate ultimately influence outcome. Not the least of these participants, of course, is the researcher and the research itself.

REFERENCES

Allman, L. (1982). The poetic mind: Further thoughts on an 'aesthetic preference.' *Family Process, 21*, 415–428.

Andreozzi, L.L. (in press). *The effects of research on practice: A child-centered family therapy outcome study.* (Tentative title), New York: Brunner/Mazel.

Campbell, D.T., & Stanley, J.C. (1963). *Experimental and quasi-experimental designs for research.* Chicago: Rand McNally.

Colapinto, G. (1979). The relative value of empirical evidence. *Family Process, 18*, 427–441.

Dell, P. (1982). In search of truth: On the way to clinical epistemology. *Family Process, 21*, 407–414.

Gurman, A.S. (1973). The effects and effectiveness of marital therapy: A review of outcome research. *Family Process, 12*, 145–170.

Gurman, A.S., & Kniskern, D.P. (1978a). Research on marital and family therapy: Progress, perspective and prospect. In S. Garfield & A. Bergin (Eds.), *Handbook of psychotherapy and behavior change* (pp. 817–901). New York: Wiley.

Gurman, A.S., & Kniskern, D.P. (1978b). Behavioral marriage therapy: II. Empirical perspectives. *Family Process, 17*, 139–148.

Gurman, A.S., & Kniskern, D.P. (1981). Outcome research: Knowns and unknowns. In A.S. Gurman & D.P. Kniskern (Eds.), *Handbook of family therapy* (pp. 742–775). New York: Brunner/Mazel.

Gurman, A.S. & Knudson, R.M. (1978). Behavioral marriage therapy: I. A psychodynamic-systems analysis and critique. *Family Process, 17*, 121–138.

Gurman, A.S., Knudson, R.M., & Kniskern, D.P. (1978). Behavioral marriage therapy: IV. Take two aspirins and call us in the morning. *Family Process 17*, 165–180.

Jacobson, N.S. (1978). A review of the research on the effectiveness of marital therapy. In T.L. Paolino & B.S. McCrady (Eds.), *Marriage and marital therapy* (pp. 395–444). New York: Brunner/Mazel.

Jacobson, N.S., & Weiss, R.L. (1978). Behavioral marriage therapy: II. The contents of Gurman et al. may be hazardous to our health. *Family Process, 17*, 149–164.

Kantor, D. (1985, February). Therapy as a cybernetic process. Keynote Address, Third Annual Conference on Family Competence, Center for Family Studies, Arizona State University.

Kantor, D., & Andreozzi, L.L. (1985). The cybernetics of family therapy and family therapy research. In J.C. Hansen (Ed.), *Family therapy collections: Vol. 15.* Integrating research and clinical practice. Rockville, MD: Aspen Systems Corporation.

Keeney, B.P. (1979). Ecosystemic epistemology: An alternative paradigm for diagnosis. *Family Process, 18*, 161–173.

Keeney, B.P. (1982a). Not pragmatics, not aesthetics. *Family Process, 21*, 429–434.

Keeney, B.P. (1982b). What is an epistemology of family therapy? *Family Process, 21*, 141–152.

Keeney, B.P., & Sprenkle, D.H. (1982). Ecosystemic epistemology: Critical implications for the aesthetics and pragmatics of family therapy. *Family Process, 21*, 1–19.

Pinsof, W.M. (1981). Family therapy and process research. In A.S. Gurman & D.P. Kniskern (Eds.), *Handbook of family therapy* (pp. 699–741). New York: Brunner/Mazel.

Todd, T., & Stanton, M.D. (1983). Research on marital and family therapy: Answers, issues, and recommendations for the future. In B. Wolman & G. Striker (Eds.), *Handbook of family and marital therapy* (pp. 91–115). New York: Plenum.

Wells, R.A., Dilkes, T., & Trivelli, N. (1972). The results of family therapy: A critical review of the literature. *Family Process, 7*, 189–207.

2

Marital and Family Therapy Research: The Meaning for the Clinician

Frederick S. Wamboldt, M.D.
University of Wisconsin Medical
School
Madison, Wisconsin

Marianne Z. Wamboldt, M.D.
University of Wisconsin Medical
School
Madison, Wisconsin

Alan S. Gurman, Ph.D.
University of Wisconsin Medical
School
Madison, Wisconsin

G ONE ARE THE DAYS IN which "it was taken for granted that a therapist and a researcher were of the same species" (Haley, 1978, pp. 73–74), when "research and therapy were fundamentally fused" (Wynne, 1983, p. 114). Indeed, at this time it appears that clinicians glean little from research, while researchers seem to pay little heed to the complexities of clinical practice. The "clinician-researcher" has become at least an endangered species, if not the proverbial "missing link." As Barlow (1982) observed, "At present, clinical research has little or no influence on clinical practice . . . [and there is] a growing acceptance of the proposition that clinicians will not do science and that very few scientists will engage in clinical practice" (pp. 147–148).

As Gurman (1983a) pointed out, there are at least five groups of potential "consumers" of family therapy research:

1. public policy makers, both government agencies and third party carriers, who want to know which of the myriad existing therapies is most effective for which clinical problems, most economical to provide, and safest to practice (Parloff, 1979).

2. families or "patients," whose concerns are similar to those of government agencies and insurance carriers, but are much more personal and immediate.

3. therapists, students of therapy, and teachers of psychotherapy who do not currently work within a systemic perspective. At least some members of this group may be influenced by clinically significant research findings.

4. theoreticians and clinicians who want to understand the mechanisms of

change in family therapy and to determine whether these mechanisms are common to all methods of treatment or are salient only within particular methods.

5. practicing clinicians and students of family therapy. This group may have the greatest potential use for research findings, for they are the experts to whom families turn for help.

It is clear that current research is more useful to some of these consumer groups than to others, but it may not be clear why family therapy research has not been of more use to the practicing clinician.

THEORETICAL PREFERENCES AND OPENNESS TO RESEARCH

Norcross and Prochaska (1983) surveyed a group of psychotherapists to determine what factors influenced their selection of a theoretical orientation. Of the 14 factors evaluated, outcome research ranked a lowly 10th. The four most influential factors were clinical experience, values and personal philosophy, graduate training, and personal life experiences. Moreover, 77% of the therapists were either ''quite satisfied'' or ''very satisfied'' with their choices. Sundland (1977) suggested a strong connection between a therapist's personality and choice of orientation, while Steiner (1978) commented rather pessimistically that ''the reason for one's choice of theoretical orientations is as ineffable as the explanation for the selection of one's spouse'' (p. 371).

Such data may help to explain the observation of Barlow (1982) that psychotherapists do not adopt an approach on the basis of its relative scientific sta-

tus. Two of the numerous possible explanations for this seem especially compelling. First, the field of family therapy has an abundance of intensely charismatic clinical teachers. Although identification with and loyalty to such figures and their respective therapeutic approaches have undoubtedly motivated many clinicians to adopt their way of working, respect for these teachers and their ideas is unlikely to preclude practicing therapists from making use of clinically meaningful research. A second explanation was suggested by Schwartz and Breunlin (1983), who reported that

> most of the clinical practitioners . . . found most [research papers] to be of little relevance to their work. . . . The picture of research that emerged was of an inaccessible domain of knowledge, which might contain something of value, but which usually seemed hopelessly remote from the experience of the clinician. (p. 24)

New research strategies are needed to close this accessibility gap (Gurman, 1983b; Gurman, Kniskern, & Pinsof, in press).

RESEARCH FINDINGS AND THEIR CLINICAL IMPLICATIONS

The general efficacy of marital and family therapy has been clearly demonstrated across different types of clinical problems and different types of therapy; beneficial outcomes are obtained in approximately two-thirds of cases. Moreover, family therapy has been found to be as effective or even more effective than other treatment approaches (Gurman & Kniskern, 1978b, 1981). Deterioration, i.e., negative outcomes, occurs in marital and family therapy with about the same frequency as in other treatment approaches (Gurman & Kniskern, 1978a), although conjoint treatment offers a significantly greater chance of positive outcome and a lesser chance of deterioration than does individual therapy for marital conflict (Gurman & Kniskern, 1978a, 1978b).

While such findings are of great interest to public policy makers and, more indirectly, to families in need of therapy, several observers of the research scene have criticized the emphasis on such "politically motivated" research (Reiss, 1984; Ryder, 1984a, 1984b). As Ryder (1984a) stated, "The goals of much outcome research . . . [have been] justification, not information" (p. 3). These critics argue that future research should be directed toward questions with "more scientific value."

Politically motivated research has failed the clinician in at least three ways. First, these studies have often been of the comparative-competitive variety (Klein & Gurman, 1981), in which Therapy A is pitted against Therapy B. Since no one method of therapy has been demonstrated to be more effective than others across a broad range of problems, few clinicians, who are generally satisfied with the services that they offer (Norcross & Prochaska, 1983), are willing to change their therapeutic approach on the basis of such studies. Research that addresses the use of one treatment modality in conjunction with others (e.g., comparison of family therapy alone, medication therapy alone, and family therapy with medication therapy for the treatment of depression [c.f., Rounsaville, Klerman, & Weissman, 1981]), may attract greater attention from clinicians. Second, the outcome

parameters used to assess change typically have not been sufficiently broad to allow clinicians to apply the results to their own practice. Gurman & Kniskern (1978a, 1978b, 1981) have proposed the use of multiperspective, multilevel, and multidimensional outcome matrices as a partial solution to this problem. For example, a report by a "behavioral" researcher that training parents in techniques to decrease aggressive behavior in a child also produces marked improvement in the parents' marriage and in the parent-grandparent relationships should be of import to a more "systemic" colleague. Third, as discussed earlier, the choice of a theoretical orientation is a very personal process. Research that offers the possibility of enhancing the efficacy, applicability, and dissemination of the therapeutic approach to which therapists are already deeply and personally committed is likely to be received more enthusiastically.

While more theoretically grounded research in family therapy is sorely needed (Gurman et al., in press), the more mundane "political" research should not be dismissed entirely. As a general rule, practicing family therapists can ply their trade with confidence that systemically grounded interventions are, indeed, powerful. Family interventions are not placebos, but family therapy has been found to be more effective than no treatment in virtually every case in which such studies have been undertaken (Gurman et al., in press).

"PUNCTUATING" THE KNOWN WORLD

It appears that two complementary, yet different, paths are needed if researchers are to close the gap with clinicians. The first path is often called school-specific research; investigators attempt to provide the long-awaited answer to Paul's (1967) question, "What therapy is most effective for what problems, treated by what therapist, according to what criteria, in what setting?" (p. 111). The second path, only recently laid down in the family field, involves efforts to identify the effective components of family therapy both within and across the various schools. Such research is the empirical arm of the burgeoning movement toward conceptual and technical integration in family therapy (e.g., Gurman, 1981; Pinsof, 1983). Since research from an integrative perspective is, as yet, exceedingly rare in published literature, this section will highlight some findings from the "school-specific" outcome literature and pose some illustrative within-school questions (cf., Kniskern & Gurman, 1981) that we see as crucial for fostering future linkages between research and practice.

Figure 1 presents a "punctuation" of many of the common marital and family treatment approaches onto two-dimensional space. While admittedly this effort as a punctuation of "reality" is arbitrary, it is presented for two purposes. First, it organizes the data that follow into clusters that may have important theoretical and practical implications. The two axes were chosen to represent what we consider to be two major dimensions of theoretical differences in the field of marital and family therapy. The first is the degree to which the therapeutic method presupposes an "accurate" reality in traditional (i.e., cause-effect, "linear," "Newtonian") terms versus an evolving reality in "systemic" (i.e., "circular,"

"Batesonian") terms. The second dimension reflects the degree to which a method postulates that change occurs as a result of presenting problem–centered, technique-based interventions (pragmatic) versus a relationship-based intervention in which the "real" problem is believed to be initially hidden ("aesthetic").

The second purpose for using this map is that it graphically portrays the hypothesis that generalization of the applicability of research findings from one school may be greater for "neighboring" schools than for more (spatially) distant schools. Given the sparse amount of data for some of the schools (Gurman et al., in press), Figure 1 may be of use both to the clinician who is evaluating the literature and to the researcher who is designing future studies.

Quadrant I: Traditional-Pragmatic: Behavioral and Psychoeducational Approaches

The behavioral approaches consist of a relatively integrated group of therapies in which the principles of social learning theory are applied to marital and family problems. The central assumption of behavioral therapists is that behavior and interaction are controlled, shaped, and maintained by events in the environment and, accordingly, can best be changed by modification of environmental contingencies. (Those who advocate behavioral marital therapy have recently shown increasing interest in the cognitive dimensions of family behavior, however.) Perhaps more often than any other group, behavioral therapists have developed systematic treatment packages, with a strong emphasis on empirical evaluation and validation of therapeutic outcomes. Although tech-

Figure 1 The Marital and Family Research World

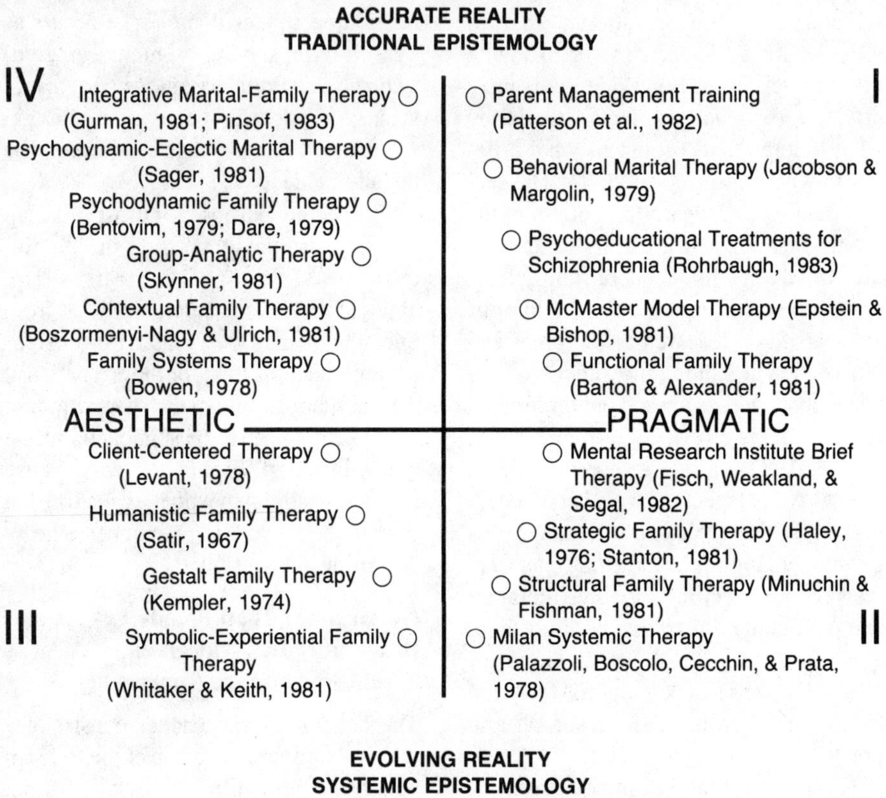

ACCURATE REALITY
TRADITIONAL EPISTEMOLOGY

IV Integrative Marital-Family Therapy ○
(Gurman, 1981; Pinsof, 1983)
Psychodynamic-Eclectic Marital Therapy ○
(Sager, 1981)
Psychodynamic Family Therapy ○
(Bentovim, 1979; Dare, 1979)
Group-Analytic Therapy ○
(Skynner, 1981)
Contextual Family Therapy ○
(Boszormenyi-Nagy & Ulrich, 1981)
Family Systems Therapy ○
(Bowen, 1978)

○ Parent Management Training   **I**
(Patterson et al., 1982)

○ Behavioral Marital Therapy (Jacobson &
Margolin, 1979)

○ Psychoeducational Treatments for
Schizophrenia (Rohrbaugh, 1983)

○ McMaster Model Therapy (Epstein &
Bishop, 1981)
○ Functional Family Therapy
(Barton & Alexander, 1981)

AESTHETIC ——————————————————**PRAGMATIC**

Client-Centered Therapy ○
(Levant, 1978)

Humanistic Family Therapy ○
(Satir, 1967)

Gestalt Family Therapy ○
(Kempler, 1974)

III   Symbolic-Experiential Family ○
Therapy
(Whitaker & Keith, 1981)

○ Mental Research Institute Brief
Therapy (Fisch, Weakland, &
Segal, 1982)
○ Strategic Family Therapy (Haley,
1976; Stanton, 1981)
○ Structural Family Therapy (Minuchin &
Fishman, 1981)
○ Milan Systemic Therapy   **II**
(Palazzoli, Boscolo, Cecchin, & Prata,
1978)

EVOLVING REALITY
SYSTEMIC EPISTEMOLOGY

nical interventions vary to some extent, treatment usually consists of some combination of (1) identification of dysfunctional behavior, (2) education in the basic principles of social learning theory, (3) communication training, (4) problem-solving skill training, and (5) contingency contracting. The effectiveness of four behavioral-psychoeducational approaches for specific clinical problems has been convincingly established (Gurman et al., in press).

Parent management training, a therapy for childhood conduct disorders, has been developed over the past two decades. Parent management training is a largely didactic procedure in which parents are trained to modify specific problematic aggressive or nonaggressive behaviors in their children within the home environment (Patterson, Reid, Jones, & Conger, 1975). The identified patient is usually a preadolescent boy, aged 3 to 12, who has been referred for outpatient treatment of conduct disorders. Parent management training has been found to be more effective than no treatment at all (Patterson, 1974a; Patterson, Chamberlain, & Reid, 1982; Patterson & Fleischman, 1979; Walter & Gilmore, 1973; Wiltz & Patterson, 1974), to have treatment effects that last up to 18 months (Fleischman & Szykula, 1981; Patterson & Fleischman, 1979), to generalize to nontargeted deviant behavior (Patterson, 1974a, 1974b) and to classroom behavior (Patterson, Cobb, & Ray, 1972), to improve the behavior of the identified patient's siblings (Arnold, Levine, & Patterson, 1975), and to decrease maternal psychopathology, especially depression (Patterson & Fleischman, 1979; Patterson & Reid, 1973). Attempts by those outside Patterson's group to replicate the results have shown more variability of outcome, however; factors such as paternal absence, low socioeconomic status, severe marital discord, parental psychopathology, and weak maternal support systems have been associated with diminished treatment gains and poorer maintenance of gains (Kazdin, 1984).

Behavioral marital therapy (Jacobson & Margolin, 1979) has been especially beneficial with moderately distressed couples and, at times, with severely distressed couples (Gurman & Kniskern, 1978b; Jacobson, 1978, 1979). While behavioral marital therapy appears to decrease negative verbal behavior consistently, it does not appear to increase positive communication consistently (Baucom & Hoffman, 1985). When Jacobson and his colleagues (Jacobson, Follette, Revenstorf, Baucom, Hahlweg, & Margolin, 1984) used a psychometrically reliable, yet very stringent, change index to reevaluate the response to behavioral marital therapy of 148 couples, they found that 54.7% of couples improved significantly, although the beneficial change was limited to one spouse in 40% of these couples. Only slightly more than one-third of the treated couples actually moved from dis-

tressed to nondistressed ratings as a consequence of behavioral marital therapy. This is consistent with the report that a substantial proportion of couples remain distressed at the end of behavioral marital therapy (Baucom & Hoffman, 1985). Some data suggest that behavioral marital therapy may be most effective with younger couples (Hahlweg, Schindler, Revenstorf, & Brengelmann, 1984; Turkewitz & O'Leary, 1981) and with couples who show a greater commitment to continuing their relationship (Beach & Broderick, 1983; Crowe, 1978; Hahlweg et al., 1984). Because Jacobson and his associates based their reanalysis of behavioral marital therapy outcomes on criteria that were much more stringent than those used to evaluate the outcomes of other marital therapies, their conclusions do not suggest that behavioral marital therapy is relatively ineffective. Instead, the kinds of couple characteristics that have been associated with better behavioral marital therapy outcomes may apply to these other marital therapies as well.

Several different behaviorally based psychoeducational treatments for schizophrenia have appeared in recent years (Berkowitz, Kuipers, Eberlein-Vries, & Leff, 1981; Falloon, Boyd, McGill, Razani, Moss, & Gildeman, 1982; Goldstein, Rodnick, Evans, May, & Steinberg, 1978). These "stress/vulnerability" family theorists suggest that there is a "core, biological deficit which makes the [schizophrenic] patient vulnerable to stressful stimulation from their environment" (Rohrbaugh, 1983, p. 30). Critical and intrusive family members are seen as an especially potent source of stress (Vaughn & Leff, 1976). The goal of treatment is to reduce the stress experienced by the schizophrenic patient by lowering the family's "emotional temperature"; this may be accomplished by means of a variety of techniques, including education about the nature, course, and prognosis of schizophrenia; concurrent administration of antipsychotic medications; modification of the relatives' expectations concerning the social and symptomatic functioning of the schizophrenic patient; concurrent multiple family support groups; and training in problem-solving and crisis management skills (Rohrbaugh, 1983).

Psychoeducational treatment of schizophrenics and their families has been shown to be more effective than is individual supportive therapy in terms of relapse rate, level of symptomatology, and social functioning (Falloon, Boyd, McGill, 1984; Falloon et al., 1982); to have an additive effect when used with antipsychotic medication treatment to reduce "negative" symptoms (e.g., withdrawal, blunted affect) that are typically refractory to medication therapy (Goldstein et al., 1978); and to be superior to outpatient antipsychotic medication therapy in a group of patients deemed high risk on the basis of their family emotional climate (Berkowitz et al., 1981; Leff, Kuipers, Berkowitz, Eberlein-Vries, & Sturgeon, 1982). These findings, although still awaiting replication, document the efficacy of this approach with a very difficult patient population. Moreover, very promising work is in progress to extend these psychoeducational approaches to other major psychiatric disorders, such as depression (C. Anderson, personal communication, 1983; Glick, 1984).

Functional family therapy (Barton & Alexander, 1981), an approach that combines behavioral methods (e.g., contingency contracting and modeling, cognitively oriented paradoxical reframing, and the facilitation of clear communication), has been applied to the treatment of soft status juvenile delinquents (e.g., runaways, curfew violators). With this population, functional family therapy has been found to be superior to individual therapy and to no therapy in a very well designed, controlled study (Alexander & Barton, 1976). In addition, it has been shown that FFT is superior to client-centered family therapy, psychodynamic-eclectic family therapy, and no treatment in terms of both the rate of recidivism among the delinquent identified patients (Parsons & Alexander, 1973) and the rate of referral of the identified patients' siblings for delinquent behavior (Klein, Alexander, & Parsons, 1977).

Clinical Implications

Apparently, a number of clinical disorders that are regularly brought to family therapists may improve significantly with treatment that explicitly focuses on the symptoms of the identified patient. The therapist should not necessarily attempt to recast the problem as fundamentally a family or marital problem (e.g., by suggesting that it is "functional" for the family).

Preliminary evidence suggests that some generalization occurs within the identified patient, both to nontarget behaviors and to target behavior in different settings. Furthermore, there may be a generalization of positive outcome to other family members in some circumstances. These and related findings on the treatment of certain adult anxiety disorders, especially agoraphobia (Gurman et al., in press), suggest that the reluctance of systemically oriented therapists to focus on the identified patient's symptomatic behavior may be greatly overdrawn, at least for some clinical problems. They also suggest that, for some disorders, clinically important effects can be achieved at other systems levels even when a symptom focus is maintained.

Research Implications

Although marital and family therapists who adhere to a behavioral and psychoeducational approach have developed more clinically relevant research than have those who advocate any other approach to family therapy, important questions remain to be addressed. For example, the generalization of treatment effects, both within identified patients and to members of their families who exhibit similar "deviant" behavior, must be more closely examined. Such generalizability, if replicated, could have major implications for treatment planning. When, as is sometimes the case, the deviant behavior rate of the identified patient is no higher than that of the patient's siblings (Arnold et al., 1975; Patterson, 1974a, 1974b), does it matter who is chosen as the identified patient? Are additive effects obtained by treating all family members with deviant behavior simultaneously? How do successful behavioral interventions with one family member affect the behavior and relationships of other family members? Perhaps, under some conditions, improvement in one sibling is associated with deterioration in another sibling or with improvement in the marital relationship.

Future research is needed to determine whether severe problem behavior can be treated with behavioral methods. With the exception of the studies on the psychoeducational treatment of schizophrenia and the work in progress on major depression, studies of behavioral therapies have not dealt with difficult, severely disturbed adult patient populations. Information on populations that respond poorly to behavioral interventions would be of particular value to clinicians who practice from within an integrative model (e.g., Gurman, 1981; Pinsof, 1983).

Behavioral therapists commonly use an assortment of techniques, all more or less derived from social learning theory. Component analyses to identify the crucial element(s) of effective treatments not only would increase the efficacy of therapy, but also might provide vital clues concerning the mechanisms of change in behavioral marital and family therapy.

Quadrant II: Systemic-Pragmatic: Structural and Strategic Approaches

The four major structural-strategic approaches (see Figure 1) have been developed rather independently, within quite different clinical contexts. They share a systemic theoretical orientation toward dysfunctional behavior, however, in that all problems are considered manifestations of family disturbances. This view has been summarized by Stanton (1981) as follows:

1) "symptoms" can be viewed simply as particular types of behavior functioning as homeostatic mechanisms which regulate family transactions (Jackson, 1957, 1965); 2) problems in an identified patient cannot be considered apart from the *context* in which they occur

and the *functions* which they serve; 3) an individual cannot be expected to change unless his family system changes (Haley, 1962); 4) "insight" per se is not a necessary prerequisite for change. (p. 365)

The structural-strategic schools differ in the way in which family data are organized. Some emphasize *structure* (e.g., power, hierarchies, alliances, and coalitions), and others emphasize *process* (e.g., family rules for communication and circuits of interaction). These schools share a rather pragmatic reliance on some combination of common intervention strategies, including in-session and between-session tasks and directives, cognitive reframing, and paradoxical interventions. The emphasis of structural-strategic therapists on the therapist's technical skills to change problematic behavior is second only to that of the behavioral therapists.

Structural-strategic approaches have been shown to be effective in treating several difficult clinical problems. Minuchin and his colleagues (Minuchin, Rosman, & Baker, 1978) have clearly delineated a model of dysfunctional family interaction that they believe to be central to the symptomatic behavior of psychosomatic children and adolescents. This model emphasizes enmeshed subsystem boundaries, parental overprotectiveness, behavioral rigidity, poor conflict resolution skills, and the symptomatic child's involvement in parental marital conflict.

Treatment with structural family therapy (Minuchin & Fishman, 1981) has been associated with and successful with children and adolescents with anorexia nervosa, diabetes mellitus, and chronic asthma (Liebman, Minuchin, Baker, & Rosman, 1974; Minuchin, Baker,

Rosman, Liebman, Milman, & Todd, 1975; Minuchin et al., 1978). Objective measures of physiological functioning (e.g., blood sugar level, respiratory function, and weight gain) and psychosocial functioning at home, at school, and with peers were used as outcome criteria. In addition, follow-up (1 to 84 months) of the individuals with anorexia showed that treatment effects were generally maintained and the rate of rehospitalization was extremely low. Unfortunately, these impressive results have yet to be fully replicated, although a preliminary report has recently suggested that a structural-strategic approach improves symptom control in bulimic females (Schwartz, Barrett, & Saba, 1984).

A great many data have been amassed concerning the effectiveness of structural-strategic family therapy in the treatment of drug abuse (Stanton, 1978; Stanton, Todd, & Associates, 1982; Stanton, Todd, Steier, Van Deusen, Marder, Rosoff, Seaman, & Skibinski, 1980; Szapocznik, Kurtines, Foote, Perez-Vidal, & Hervis, 1983). In the most sophisticated of the studies, a group of male heroin addicts who received structural-strategic family therapy after each had made at least two prior attempts to detoxify showed more improvement on a variety of drug use measures than did control groups who did not receive family therapy (Stanton, Todd, & Associates, 1982). Expected treatment gains in psychosocial areas (specifically, employment status and school enrollment) were not achieved, however.

When Stanton and his colleagues analyzed videotapes of family interactions obtained before and after treatment, they found the degree of change in certain family processes (e.g., the ability to make decisions and the ability to resolve conflicts) to be highly correlated with drug use measures. This research constitutes perhaps the first empirical validation of a central systemic construct, namely, the relationship between changes in symptoms and changes in family interaction.

Clinical Implications

It appears that structural-strategic therapies can produce impressive symptomatic improvement with a number of difficult clinical problems that have traditionally had a very poor prognosis. In fact, these therapies may be the family treatments of choice for substance abuse and psychosomatic disorders. Structural-strategic therapies are rarely "pure" in practice, however, and may regularly include treatment interventions borrowed from other treatment methods (Todd, in press), such as behavioral problem solving and communication skills training. The clinician should not view the use of such techniques as compromising adherence to a structural-strategic orientation, but as synergistically enhancing the potency of "standard" structural-strategic interventions.

The evidence that suggests an association between change in the identified patient's symptoms and change in the family's interactions does not establish a direct causality. Therefore, the clinician must maintain a focus on both the symptomatic behavior of the identified patient and the family interactional context within which such behavior occurs.

Research Implications

A crucial need for the future is a comprehensive assessment of the effects that changes in the symptomatic individual induce in other family members and fam-

ily relationships. Symptom bearer substitution and homeostatic deterioration of other relationships within the family, for example, are hypotheses that have a long history in the systemically oriented literature and could be validated empirically.

As noted earlier, structural-strategic therapists use a wide variety of interventions, some specific to their respective schools, others borrowed from other therapeutic methods. In view of the array of technically compatible interventions available to therapists, component analyses to determine effective and/or essential treatment ingredients are needed.

Some structural-strategic therapists seem to play down the role of therapist factors (e.g., ability to manage a therapist-patient relationship) and to emphasize the importance of technical skills. Studies of the role of "nonspecific" therapist characteristics could clarify which characteristics are essential for use of the structural-strategic approaches and help to predict which candidates are suitable for training in these methods.

Finally, the use of paradoxical techniques warrants much closer scrutiny. These techniques are generally considered quite potent. Like medications and surgical scalpels, they can produce impressive successes when applied correctly and significant harm if improperly used. While clinical guidelines have been suggested for the use of paradoxical interventions (Haley, 1976; Papp, 1980; Stanton, 1981), the development of empirically validated guidelines is crucial for optimal efficiency and safety.

Quadrants III and IV: Aesthetic-Intergenerational-Experiential Approaches

The systemic-aesthetic and traditional-aesthetic schools of marital and family therapy can be considered together as the intergenerational-experiential approaches. Those who have adopted these approaches typically view dysfunctional behavior as the result of family level developmental fixation, such as insufficient differentiation from or excessive bonds of obligation to the respective families of origin. Individual symptom bearers are believed to hold an "elected office" (Whitaker & Keith, 1981, p. 196) and to play roles orchestrated to a multigenerational score. Symptoms are thought to appear when some new stress (e.g., the first child's departure from home, the death of the father) cannot be surmounted because of the family's developmental fixation. In this context, the presenting problem is not considered the "real" problem to be addressed in therapy.

The therapist's influence is believed to derive primarily from his or her personal qualities, not from technical skill, and the outcome of the therapeutic experience is seen as greatly dependent on the therapists's interpersonal skills. The therapeutic goal is to promote a healing, affective experience. Techniques are of varying importance and may include taking a history, facilitating communication, clarifying family patterns and boundaries, and sharing or modeling fantasy/play experiences. Insight alone is usually not considered sufficient for change.

Although there is a paucity of empirical studies on these approaches, two recent, related studies offer some evidence of the efficacy of certain experiential approaches. Johnson and Greenberg (in press[a]) randomly assigned 45 couples with complaints of marital dis-

turbance to emotionally focused couples therapy (i.e., therapy that emphasizes the role of affect and intrapsychic experience), cognitive behavioral marital therapy, or a wait-list control group. After 8 weeks of treatment provided by experienced therapists, both treatment groups showed significant gains over the control group. In addition, the emotionally focused couples therapy was more effective than was the cognitive behavioral therapy, as determined by measures of marital adjustment, intimacy, and target complaint reduction. The superior effect of the emotionally focused treatment on marital adjustment persisted at 8-week follow-up. In a partial replication, the initial wait-list couples were given eight sessions of emotionally focused couples therapy (Johnson & Greenberg, in press[b]). While significant improvement was noted on most outcome measures, the measured effect size was less than one-half that in the original study. The use of novice therapists in this replication may have been partly responsible for the diminished treatment benefits.

Clinical Implications

The studies done by Johnson and Greenberg (in press [a, b]), plus the more broadly based observations of Gurman and his associates (in press) on the efficacy of psychodynamically oriented couples therapy, suggest that clinicians should reconsider the effective components of family therapy in general. While it has become fashionable for family therapists to dismiss the treatment relevance of the conscious and unconscious processes within an individual family member, a truly systemic orientation to clinical work requires therapists to assess and potentially to intervene at multiple levels of human experience. Intrapersonal processes are as much a domain for systemically oriented therapeutic intervention as are interpersonal processes.

Research Implications

Outcome research in the intergenerational-experiential field poses significant difficulties because of the multiple factors involved. The centrality of the therapist's personality and interpersonal skills, the degree of abstraction in the assumptions of the various schools (e.g., the concept of differentiation in family systems therapy [Bowen, 1978]), and the lack of well-articulated methods and theoretical tenets, for example, all make it difficult to bring well-designed, clinically meaningful research to fruition. Nonetheless, there are several areas of exploration that may prove useful to clinicians.

Since the theoretical world of the intergenerational-experiential therapies is significantly different from that of the behavioral-psychoeducational and structural-strategic approaches, the possibility that the various approaches have a differential effectiveness with different clinical problems merits further study. In addition, the question of whether certain therapist personality traits are associated with greater success should be explored. While the therapist's experience level, structuring skills, and relationship skills have been shown to correlate with treatment outcome regardless of the therapist's orientation (Kniskern & Gurman, 1979), these factors may be of particular salience for the outcomes of the intergenerational-experiential approaches.

Training in the intergenerational-experiential approaches is notoriously difficult and consists primarily of experiential activities, such as small group experiences, work with one's own family of origin, personal psychotherapy, and apprenticeships with ''master'' therapists. Research aimed at improving the efficacy of training in these approaches (e.g., studying the relative effectiveness of various training activities in different combinations and at different training times) is certain to benefit both clinicians and future researchers.

Divorce Therapy

Separation and divorce are prevalent phenomena of significant social consequence that are regularly dealt with by all family therapists. Divorce therapy focuses on the structural, interactional, and/or psychological consequences of marital dissolution. Its methods are not confined to those of any single school of marital or family therapy, but some clinical guidelines have been proposed for various dissolution-oriented treatments.

Several divorce-oriented treatment formats have been commonly used in clinical practice (Sprenkle & Storm, 1983). Group therapy for divorced individuals has yielded rather consistently positive outcomes, with the most commonly studied dependent variable being self-esteem. Separation counseling, although probably used clinically with some frequency, has not yet been the object of clinical research.

The divorce-related intervention that has been studied most frequently and reliably is divorce mediation. In all mediation studies to date, mediation has been associated with a higher rate of pre-trial agreements; a greater level of satisfaction with the agreements; major reductions in the amount of litigation after final court orders; an increase in joint custody agreements; and, with one exception, decreases in public expenses, such as custody studies and court costs.

Clinical Implications

Data from existing mediation studies have been used to formulate a clinically useful description of those couples for whom mediation is likely to be successful:

> The ideal candidates are couples mediating around a limited number of issues, for whom the level of conflict is moderate, and in which both spouses feel able to represent themselves in the negotiations. Both accept the divorce and have begun the process of "letting go." The mediation occurs early in the dissolution process and before receiving court orders (either temporary or permanent). There are no third parties significantly involved in the dispute. Both parties sense some ability to communicate and cooperate with the other. Money is not a major issue in the divorce, and there are adequate resources to carry on as a single person. Finally, the attorneys support the mediation process. (Sprenkle & Storm, 1983, p. 250)

CONCLUSION

Although the family therapy research literature now contains several hundred studies, relatively few clinically reliable guidelines can be gleaned from this vast mass of data. Nonetheless, those that can be drawn from these data with some confidence are not at all trivial. Of particular significance is the fact that, while several of the clinical implications are quite consistent with prevalent wisdom and lore, several others challenge some widely held, or at least vociferously argued, views in the field.

Moreover, as Gurman and his associates (in press) have recently noted, "proponents of most of the major methods of family and marital therapy have thus far produced little or no empirical evidence of the effectiveness of their treatments, and the proponents of most of the remaining major methods as a group have provided only slightly more." Furthermore, they showed that, of the 150 combinations of the 15 major family therapy methods and the 10 most commonly investigated clinical disorders and problems, only 35 (or 23%) have been studied at all and evidence of at least probable effectiveness has been put forth for only 13 (9%). While these findings may well cause some concern among family therapists, all is not so bleak as it first appears. Gurman and his colleagues (in press) emphasized that, "when family methods have been rigorously tested, they have been found to be effective without exception."

It is necessary to work toward making research consistent with the theoretical assumptions of the various family therapies (Gurman et al., in press) and more responsive to the questions and concerns of the practicing family clinician. Research should be guided by solid clinical theory, and clinical practice should be guided by solid research. Still, clinical theory will not raise all the questions that require empirical scrutiny, nor will research provide guidance on all matters of practical concern. An open dialogue between clinicians and researchers is essential to maximize the gains that can be achieved in both domains.

REFERENCES

Alexander, J.F., & Barton, C. (1976). Behavioral systems therapy for families. In D.H. Olson (Ed.), *Treating relationships*. Lake Mills, IA: Graphic.

Arnold, J.E., Levine, A.G., & Patterson, G.P. (1975). Changes in sibling behavior following family intervention. *Journal of Consulting and Clinical Psychology, 43*, 683–688.

Barlow, D.H. (1982). On the relation of clinical research to clinical practice: Current issues, new directions. *Journal of Consulting and Clinical Psychology, 49*, 147–155.

Barton, C., & Alexander, J.F. (1981). Functional family therapy. In A. Gurman & D. Kniskern (Eds.), *Handbook of family therapy*. New York: Brunner/Mazel.

Baucom, D.H., & Hoffman, J.A. (1985). The effectiveness of marital therapy: Current status and applications to the clinical setting. In N. Jacobson & A. Gurman (Eds.), *Clinical handbook of marital therapy*. New York: Guilford.

Beach, S.R., & Broderick, J.E. (1983). Commitment: A variable in women's response to marital therapy. *American Journal of Family Therapy, 11*, 16–24.

Bentovim, A. (1979). Towards creating a focal hypothesis for brief focal family therapy. *Journal of Family Therapy, 1*, 125–136.

Berkowitz, R., Kuipers, L., Eberlein-Vries, R., & Leff, J.P. (1981). Lowering expressed emotion in relatives. In M. Goldstein (Ed.), *New developments in interventions with families of schizophrenics*. San Francisco: Jossey-Bass.

Boszormenyi-Nagy, I., & Ulrich, D. (1981). Contextual family therapy. In A. Gurman & D. Kniskern (Eds.), *Handbook of family therapy*. New York: Brunner/Mazel.

Bowen, M. (1978). *Family therapy in clinical practice*. New York: Jason Aronson.

Crowe, M.J. (1978). Conjoint marital therapy: A controlled outcome study. *Psychological Medicine, 8*, 623–636.

Dare, C. (1979). Psychoanalysis and systems in family therapy. *Journal of Family Therapy, 1*, 137–151.

Epstein, N.B., & Bishop, D.S. (1981). Problem-centered systems therapy of the family. In A.

Gurman & D. Kniskern (Eds.), *Handbook of family therapy*. New York: Brunner/Mazel.

Falloon, I.R.H., Boyd, J.L., & McGill, C.W. (1984). *Family care of schizophrenia*. New York: Guilford.

Falloon, I.R.H., Boyd, J.L., McGill, C.W., Razani, J., Moss, H.B., & Gildeman, A.M. (1982). Family management in the prevention of exacerbations of schizophrenia. *New England Journal of Medicine, 306*, 1437–1440.

Fisch, R., Weakland, J.H., & Segal, L. (1982). *The tactics of change: Doing therapy briefly*. San Francisco: Jossey-Bass.

Fleishman, M., & Szykula, S.A. (1981). A community setting replication of a social learning treatment for aggressive children. *Behavior Therapy, 12*, 115–122.

Glick, I. (1984, June). *Inpatient family intervention: A controlled evaluation of practice. Preliminary results of the six-month followup*. Paper presented at the meeting of the American Family Therapy Association, New York.

Goldstein, M., Rodnick, E., Evans, J.R., May, P.R.A., & Steinberg, M.R. (1978). Drug and family therapy in the aftercare of acute schizophrenics. *Archives of General Psychiatry, 35*, 1169–1177.

Gurman, A.S. (1981). Integrative marital therapy: Towards the development of an interpersonal approach. In S.H. Budman (Ed.), *Forms of brief therapy*. New York: Guilford.

Gurman, A.S. (1983a). Family therapy research and the "new epistemology." *Journal of Marital and Family Therapy, 9*, 227–234.

Gurman, A.S. (1983b, July). *Psychotherapy research and the practice of psychotherapy*. Presidential Address, Society for Psychotherapy Research, Sheffield, England.

Gurman, A.S., & Kniskern, D.P. (1978a). Deterioration in marital and family therapy: Empirical, clinical and conceptual issues. *Family Process, 17*, 3–20.

Gurman, A.S., & Kniskern, D.P. (1978b). Research on family therapy: Progress, perspective and prospect. In S.L. Garfield & A.E. Bergin (Eds.), *Handbook of psychotherapy and behavior change* (2nd ed.). New York: Wiley.

Gurman, A.S., & Kniskern, D.P. (1981). Family therapy outcome research: Knowns and unknowns. In A. Gurman & D. Kniskern (Eds.), *Handbook of family therapy*. New York: Brunner/Mazel.

Gurman, A.S., Kniskern, D.P., & Pinsof, W.M. (in press). Research on the process and outcome of marital and family therapy. In S.L. Garfield & A.E. Bergin (Eds.), *Handbook of psychotherapy and behavior change* (3rd ed.). New York: Wiley.

Hahlweg, K., Schindler, L., Revenstorf, D., & Brengelmann, J.C. (1984). The Munich marital therapy study. In K. Hahlweg & N.S. Jacobson (Eds.), *Marital interaction: Analysis and modification*. New York: Guilford Press.

Haley, J. (1962). Whither family therapy. *Family Process, 1,* 69–100.

Haley, J. (1976). *Problem solving therapy*. San Francisco: Jossey-Bass.

Haley, J. (1978). Ideas which handicap therapists. In M. Berger (Ed.), *Beyond the double bind*. New York: Brunner/Mazel.

Jackson, D.D. (1957). The question of family homeostasis. *Psychiatric Quarterly Supplement, 31,* 79–90.

Jackson, D.D. (1965). A suggestion for the technical handling of paranoid patients. *Psychiatry, 26,* 306–307.

Jacobson, N.S. (1978). A review of the research on the effectiveness of marital therapy. In T.J. Paolino & B.S. McCrady (Eds.), *Marriage and marital therapy: Psychoanalytic behavioral and systems theory perspectives*. New York: Brunner/Mazel.

Jacobson, N.S. (1979). Behavioral treatments for marital discord: A critical appraisal. In M. Hersen, R.M. Eisler, & P.M. Miller (Eds.), *Progress in behavior modification* (Vol. 7). New York: Academic Press.

Jacobson, N.S., Follette, W.C., Revenstorf, D., Baucom, D.H., Hahlweg, K., & Margolin, G. (1984). Variability in outcome and clinical significance of behavioral marital therapy: A reanalysis of outcome data. *Journal of Consulting and Clinical Psychology, 52,* 497–504.

Jacobson, N.S., & Margolin, G. (1979). *Marital therapy: Strategies based on social learning and behavior exchange principles*. New York: Brunner/Mazel.

Johnson, S.M., & Greenberg, L.S. (in press[a]). The differential effects of experiential and problem-solving interventions in resolving marital conflict. *Journal of Consulting and Clinical Psychology*.

Johnson, S.M., & Greenberg, L.S. (in press[b]). Emotionally focused couples therapy: An outcome study. *Journal of Marital and Family Therapy*.

Kazdin, A.E. (1984). Treatment of conduct disorders. In J.R. Williams & R. Spitzer (Eds.), *Psychotherapy research: Where are we and where should we go?* New York: Guilford.

Kempler, W. (1974). *Principles of Gestalt family therapy*. Salt Lake City: Deseret Press.

Klein, M.H., & Gurman, A.S. (1981). Ritual and reality: Some clinical implications of experimental design. In L. Rehm (Ed.), *Behavior therapy for depression*. New York: Academic Press.

Klein, N.C., Alexander, J.F., & Parsons, B.V. (1977). Impact of family systems intervention on recidivism and sibling delinquency: A model of primary prevention and program evaluation. *Journal of Consulting and Clinical Psychology, 45,* 469–474.

Kniskern, D.P., & Gurman, A.S. (1979). Research on training in marriage and family therapy: Status, issues and directions. *Journal of Marital and Family Therapy, 5,* 83–89.

Kniskern, D.P., & Gurman, A.S. (1981). Advances and prospects for family therapy research. In J.P. Vincent (Ed.), *Advances in family intervention, assessment and theory: An annual compilation of research*. Greenwich, CT: JAI Press.

Leff, J.P., Kuipers, L., Berkowitz, R., Eberlein-Vries, R., & Sturgeon, D. (1982). A controlled trial of social intervention in the families of schizophrenic patients. *British Journal of Psychiatry, 141,* 121–134.

Levant, R.F. (1978). Family therapy: A client-centered perspective. *Journal of Marriage and Family Counseling, 4,* 35–42.

Liebman, R., Minuchin, S., Baker, L., & Rosman, B. (1974). An integrated treatment program for anorexia nervosa. *American Journal of Psychiatry, 131,* 432–436.

Minuchin, S., Baker, L., Rosman, B., Liebman, R., Milman, L., & Todd, T. (1975). A conceptual model of psychosomatic illness in children:

Family organization and family therapy. *Archives of General Psychiatry, 32,* 1031–1038.

Minuchin, S., & Fishman, H.C. (1981). *Family therapy techniques.* Cambridge, MA: Harvard University Press.

Minuchin, S., Rosman, B., & Baker, L. (1978). *Psychosomatic families: Anorexia nervosa in context.* Cambridge, MA: Harvard University Press.

Norcross, J.C., & Prochaska, J.O. (1983). Clinicians' theoretical orientations: Selection, utilization, and efficacy. *Professional Psychology, 14,* 197–208.

Palazzoli, M.S., Boscolo, L., Cecchin, G., & Prata, G. (1978). *Paradox and counterparadox: A new model in the therapy of the family in schizophrenic transaction.* New York: Jason Aronson.

Papp, P. (1980). The Greek chorus and other techniques of family therapy. *Family Process, 19,* 45–58.

Parloff, M.B. (1979). Can psychotherapy research guide the policy-maker? A little knowledge may be a dangerous thing. *American Psychologist, 34,* 296–306.

Parsons, B.V., & Alexander, J.F. (1973). Short term family intervention: A therapy outcome study. *Journal of Consulting and Clinical Psychology, 41,* 195–201.

Patterson, G.R. (1974a). Interventions for boys with conduct problems: Multiple settings, treatments, and criteria. *Journal of Consulting and Clinical Psychology, 42,* 471–481.

Patterson, G.R. (1974b). Retraining of aggressive boys by their parents: Review of recent literature and follow-up evaluation. *Canadian Psychiatric Association Journal, 19,* 142–161.

Patterson, G.R., Chamberlain, P., & Reid, J.B. (1982). A comparative evaluation of a parent-training program. *Behavior Therapy, 13,* 638–650.

Patterson, G.R., Cobb, J.A., & Ray, R.S. (1972). A social engineering technology for retraining the families of aggressive boys. In H.E. Adams & I.P. Unikel (Eds.), *Issues and trends in behavior therapy.* Springfield, IL: Charles C Thomas.

Patterson, G.R., & Fleischman, M. (1979). Maintenance of treatment effects: Some considerations concerning family systems and follow-up data. *Behavior Therapy, 10,* 168–173.

Patterson, G.R., & Reid, J. (1973). Interventions for families of aggressive boys: A replication study. *Behavior Research and Therapy, 11,* 383–394.

Patterson, G.R., Reid, J.B., Jones, R.R., & Conger, R.E. (1975). *A social learning approach to family intervention: Families with aggressive children* (Vol. 1). Eugene, OR: Castalia.

Paul, G.L. (1967). Strategy of outcome research in psychotherapy. *Journal of Consulting and Clinical Psychology, 31,* 109–118.

Pinsof, W.M. (1983). Integrative problem-centered therapy: Toward the synthesis of family and individual psychotherapies. *Journal of Marital and Family Therapy, 9,* 19–35.

Reiss, D. (1984, January). *Theoretical versus tactical inferences or how to do family psychotherapy research without dying of boredom.* Paper presented at the NIMH Conference on the State of the Art in Family Therapy Research, Rockville, MD.

Rohrbaugh, M. (1983). Schizophrenia research: Swimming against the mainstream. *Family Therapy Networker, 7,* 29–31, 61–62.

Rounsaville, B.J., Klerman, G.L., & Weissman, M.M. (1981). Do psychotherapy and pharmacotherapy for depression conflict? Empirical evidence from a clinical trial. *Archives of General Psychiatry, 38,* 24–29.

Ryder, R.G. (1984a). *Coherent diversity: Views and recommendations following the NIMH/FP workshop on efficacy research in family therapy.* Unpublished manuscript, University of Connecticut.

Ryder, R.G. (1984b, January). *The holy grail: Proven efficacy in family therapy.* Paper presented at the NIMH Conference on the State of the Art in Family Therapy Research, Rockville, MD.

Sager, C.J. (1981). Couples contracts and marital therapy. In A. Gurman & D. Kniskern (Eds.), *Handbook of family therapy.* New York: Brunner/Mazel.

Satir, V. (1967). *Conjoint family therapy.* Palo Alto, CA: Science and Behavior Books.

Schwartz, R.C., Barrett, M.J., & Saba, G. (1984, October). *Family therapy for bulimia.* Paper presented at the Annual Conference of the American Association for Marriage and Family Therapy, Washington, DC.

Schwartz, R.C., & Breunlin, D. (1983). Research: Why clinicians should bother with it. *Family Therapy Networker, 7,* 23–27, 57–59.

Skynner, A.C.R. (1981). An open-systems, group-analytic approach to family therapy. In A. Gurman & D. Kniskern (Eds.), *Handbook of family therapy.* New York: Brunner/Mazel.

Sprenkle, D.H., & Storm, C.L. (1983). Divorce therapy outcome research: A substantial and methodological review. *Journal of Marital and Family Therapy, 9,* 239–258.

Stanton, M.D. (1978). Some outcome results and aspects of structural family therapy with drug addicts. In D. Smith, S. Anderson, M. Buxton, T. Chung, N. Gottlieb, & W. Harvey (Eds.), *A multicultural view of drug abuse: Selected proceedings of the national drug abuse conference—1977.* Cambridge, MA: Schenkman.

Stanton, M.D. (1981). Strategic approaches to family therapy. In A. Gurman & D. Kniskern (Eds.), *Handbook of family therapy.* New York: Brunner/Mazel.

Stanton, M.D., Todd, T.C., & Associates. (1982). *The family therapy of drug abuse and addiction.* New York: Guilford.

Stanton, M.D., Todd, T.C., Steier, F., Van Deusen, J.M., Marder, L., Rosoff, R.J., Seaman, S.F., & Skibinski, E. (1980). *Family characteristics and family therapy of heroin addicts: Final report 1974–1978* (Grant No. R01 DA 01119). Report prepared for the National Institute on Drug Abuse, Philadelphia.

Steiner, G.L. (1978). A survey to identify factors in therapists' selection of a theoretical orientation. *Psychotherapy: Theory, Research and Practice, 15,* 371–374.

Sundland, D.M. (1977). Theoretical orientations of psychotherapists. In A.S. Gurman & A.M. Razin (Eds.), *Effective psychotherapy.* New York: Pergamon.

Szapocznik, J., Kurtines, W.M., Foote, F.H., Perez-Vidal, A., & Hervis, O. (1983). Conjoint versus one-person family therapy: Some evidence for the effectiveness of conducting family therapy through one person. *Journal of Consulting and Clinical Psychology, 51,* 889–899.

Todd, T.C. (in press). Structural/strategic marital therapy. In N.S. Jacobson & A.S. Gurman (Eds.), *Clinical handbook of marital therapy.* New York: Guilford.

Turkewitz, H., & O'Leary, K.D. (1981). A comparative outcome study of behavioral marital therapy and communication therapy. *Journal of Marital and Family Therapy, 7,* 159–169.

Vaughn, C.E., & Leff, J.P. (1976). The influence of family and social factors on the course of psychiatric illness: A comparison of schizophrenic and depressed neurotic patients. *British Journal of Psychiatry, 129,* 125–137.

Walter, H.I., & Gilmore, S.K. (1973). Placebo versus social learning effects in parent training procedures designed to alter the behavior of aggressive boys. *Behavior Therapy, 4,* 361–377.

Whitaker, C.A., & Keith, D.V. (1981). Symbolic-experiential family therapy. In A. Gurman & D. Kniskern (Eds.), *Handbook of family therapy.* New York: Brunner/Mazel.

Wiltz, N.A., & Patterson, G.R. (1974). An evaluation of parent training procedures designed to alter inappropriate aggressive behavior of boys. *Behavior Therapy, 5,* 215–221.

Wynne, L.C. (1983). Family research and family therapy: A reunion? *Journal of Marital and Family Therapy, 9,* 113–118.

3

Toward a Cybernetic Methodology of Family Therapy Research: Fitting Research Methods to Family Practice

Frederick Steier, Ph.D
Temple University
Philadelphia, Pennsylvania
and
University of Pennsylvania
Philadelphia, Pennsylvania
and
Institute of Psychology
University of Oslo
Oslo, Norway

THERE HAS BEEN, IN RECENT years, a shift in the way that family therapy is conducted. There has been, however, no corresponding shift in the way that the effectiveness of family therapy is assessed. More specifically, family therapy has been in the vanguard in both the acceptance and furtherance of ideas from what has been termed "the new epistemology" (Hoffman, 1981), which has allowed therapists to view families and therapeutic systems from a cybernetic perspective. As a basis for a theory of interventions, this cybernetic perspective has certain consequences for the evaluation of therapy outcome, but these have yet to be realized. There is, thus, a mismatch between the methods that are used in the performance of family therapy and the methods that are used to evaluate the success of the programs within which family therapy occurs. This mismatch has a strong bearing on the meaning often created from family therapy outcome studies. To improve the fit between research and therapy, several ideas need to be developed. These ideas are, to a large extent, overlapping, even though they will be presented as separate. They should be thought of as interconnected parts of a whole.

THE TRADITIONAL ASSUMPTIONS

The traditional model used in research on the effectiveness of family therapy has as its basis a particular set of assumptions that may be either stated explicitly or embedded implicitly within the research program. These assumptions, which form the underlying paradigm of the research (Kuhn, 1962; Morgan, 1983a), define the world view of the researcher. Much research in family therapy has

27

accepted a particular set of guiding assumptions without question or without any real acknowledgment. For example, they may assume that (1) the world is made up of objective and independently existing rules and relationships that may be uncovered by a noninterfering observer; (2) relationships and systems can be subjected to measurements that form a basis for an assessment of change in these relationships and systems; and (3) observations are replicable with controlled variation and can, thus, be compared across situations. Using these assumptions, researchers are forever trying to identify the precise rules of the external world. This positivist approach to science has often been seen as necessary for "good" outcome research.

Such assumptions reveal themselves in the measurement scales used to assess change and in the kinds of research designs employed to determine the relative success of a set of interventions. In order to pinpoint exactly the best explanation for differences in outcome, these research designs attempt to control variations across a set of interventions. For example, in order to compare the effectiveness of family therapy to that of a non–family therapy intervention in the treatment of families with an alcohol-abusing father, the researcher may try to eliminate every other possible difference between the families randomly assigned to the two different interventions in order to ensure that any difference in effectiveness is attributable only to that family therapy/non–family therapy distinction. If the assumption that the social world is a system of objectively determinable regularities is challenged, however, problems arise in the criteria ordinarily used to evaluate research based on such methods (Morgan, 1983b). Thus, the meaning of research such as that on the effectiveness of family therapy is often imposed through the methodology used and the measures constructed, rather than emerging from the research itself. The use of a methodology based on the principles of cybernetics will allow meaning that is more consistent with the interventions being enacted to emerge from such research.

THE CYBERNETIC CONNECTION

Principles of cybernetics have been used for some time now to guide how therapists see families and develop approaches to treatment. This connection can be traced to the work of Bateson and his colleagues (Bateson, Jackson, Haley, & Weakland, 1956), which enabled family therapists and researchers to see the location of problems in the circular patterns of interaction within a larger system (i.e., the family), rather than solely within the individual. Since that time, key ideas have included systems of feedback patterns, both negative and positive; self-regulation, usually in the form of a family homeostasis; and the processes of morphostasis and morphogenesis. This cybernetic connection for family therapy has been well documented (Hoffman, 1981).

The definition of cybernetics usually cited in this context can be traced to Wiener (1948), who described cybernetics as the study of control and communication in animal (or man) and machine. Cybernetics as a metadiscipline is itself constantly evolving, however, and it may be better defined today as the study of the process of organization in observed and observing systems, and its inherent circularities (Steier, 1985). A second-order cybernetics has emerged that, in contrast to a first-order cybernetics (i.e., the study of *observed* systems), focuses on the *observing* systems (von Foerster, 1981). This shift makes the *way* that the therapists or researchers *see* themselves become part of the therapy research process; the responsibilities emanating from the purposes of the observer (here, the therapy researcher) must be admitted (von Foerster, 1979).

Several concerns have arisen with the shift in focus from observed to observing systems. First, we must realize that the world as we know it is constructed by us, we cannot separate the phenomena we attempt to know from our systems of knowing. Von Glasersfeld (1984) has called the foundation for this view radical constructivism. Second, descriptions of observed systems must be seen in a new light. In order to understand a system, such as a family, it is necessary to focus on that system not as passive and receiving an input which leads to an output (an input–output system), but rather as an active one that is internally coherent, and autonomous (organizationally closed) (Maturana, 1978). This shift has been described by Varela (1984) as the *autonomous systems paradigm*.

CONSTRUCTION OF THE PRESENTING PROBLEM

In order to assess the effectiveness of a family intervention, the basis for the point for which the family starts its treatment must be ascertained. This is usually identified as the presenting problem. The resolution of the presenting problem is a primary goal of therapy, for a family systemic change that allows the present-ing problem to remain within the family's domain satisfies no one (Todd & Stanton, 1983).

An individual research program often has as its basis a single presenting problem (e.g., an anorectic child) or a well-defined class of presenting problems (e.g., developmental disabilities). The specification of the presenting problem is thus necessary for a particular research program if one wants to identify the domain of problems for which family therapy might be judged successful.

The presenting problem is invariably seen as an objective piece of data about a family. We must question the very notion of objectivity and treat what we ordinarily refer to as objective data as elements of our (socially) constructed world.

From a radical constructivist perspective, however, the presenting problem is not a "data point" that can be identified objectively and separated from the initial clinical interview. The presenting problem (and its value, or severity) is not merely a point of departure to be taken for granted—it is a researchable question. This is not just a theoretical distinction, but one that has very strong implications for clinical practice in terms of how data are elicited in initial interviews, where those data lie, and what they mean.

Frankel (1985) clearly illustrated this point. Working with videotapes in a conversation analysis framework, Frankel compared the discourse of a series of clinical interviews with the texts (in this case, medical records) produced from those interviews. A significant difference was observed between the concerns expressed by the patient (as identified by the researcher-observer) and those recorded by the clinician. In addition, certain types of voiced concerns (e.g., biomedical) were more likely to be recorded. Even for those items recorded, a disparity emerged between the way in which a concern was initially reported and the way in which it was entered as text. It can be concluded from this research that the medical forms themselves from which labels for presenting problems are constructed create a context for the interaction taking place. This point is even more true of research programs that "help" researchers create the classification schemata on which initial clinical interviews are based.

An obvious practical implication that can be drawn from this research is that data such as presenting problems can be viewed as matters of negotiation, controlled in part by the questions and manner of the interviewer. Interviewers must be aware of their role in the data-gathering process and in the construction of the presenting problem. The issue is not one of unobtrusive and objective interviewing, but of interviewers' awareness of their distinctions that guide the interview process and their own stated or unstated intentions; they must be aware of the way in which the presenting problem is socially constructed.

THERAPY-RESEARCH FIT AND SYSTEMIC CHANGE

The various schools of family therapy have long prided themselves on theories that allow clinicians to see problems as embedded in larger systems of cyclical interaction (i.e., the family) rather than as confined to individuals. Techniques for intervening with the family as a transactional system (in Dewey & Bentley's (1949) sense) and allowing the family to

break homeostatic cycles have been hallmarks of successful family therapy. These developments have not been matched, however, in the way in which the efficacy of such interventions is assessed.

Of primary importance is the assessment of change in the cyclical patterning of behavior in many "problem" families. It is necessary to determine whether, following therapy, a family has escaped from its dysfunctional cycle or merely moved along to another point within the usual cycle. This question is analogous to Ashby's (1956) distinction between a system's change in a way of behaving and a change within a line of behavior, a distinction that constitutes a fundamental difference between first- and second-order change (c.f., Watzlawick, Weakland, & Fisch, 1974). With or without therapy, families often move from one state of behavior to another within the same general cycle of behavior. For example, during the course of a cycle, opiate addicts may move from "using" drugs to not "using" drugs and back again (Stanton et al., 1978). An apparent change in the presenting problem in these cases may, in actuality, be related to the time at which the observations occur. Thus, a change in the family at one point after therapy's completion in no way proves that it has removed itself from its cycle.

The problem in any family therapy assessment is to develop a methodology that allows the researcher to see what type of change has taken place. This requires as a minimum:

1. studies of the process of change in families, rather than simple pre- to post-treatment assessment

2. a sensitivity to whether the change is merely an isomorphism of the previous cycle, such as a simple symptom substitution (e.g., alcohol abuse replacing opiate addiction) or system substitution (e.g., younger brother replacing older brother as opiate addict)
3. evaluation of the process of change in the family as an interactional system

Insofar as family therapy researchers talk of removing the symptom by changing the system and yet insist on evaluating the efficacy of an intervention by studying primarily the removal of the symptom (with other changes as, at best, adjunct), an examination of the process of change is of special importance.

Fisher (1982) noted that many family therapy researchers, although working from transactional theories of the family, often use methods that isolate individual members to assess those families. Fisher rightfully cited the complexity of good transactional research as a possible reason for this disparity; the issue lies not only in the complexity of the family as a system, however, but in the way that the assessment of change is performed. There is a major difference between (1) research done by those who look at the process of change in a family (or therapeutic) system at a level consonant with that system, and (2) research done by those who merely assess standardized variables that show change and then try to piece them together to re-create the complexity of the family system. The first approach makes it possible to study the changing family from both a symbolic (in the sense of the family as a meaning-creating system) and a transactional perspective, as well as to take into account the family's own coherence and autonomy.

FAMILIES AS AUTONOMOUS SYSTEMS

Many of those in the helping professions, even practitioners and researchers who recognize the systemic nature of problems, have worked from an assumption that help (in the form of aid or therapy) is done to or performed on an individual or a group of individuals. Partly to counteract this position, Krippendorff and Steier (1979) delineated three distinctions, framed as questions, that are useful in applying the principles of cybernetics to therapeutic systems:

1. Does the therapist see problems as located in parts of the system, such as individuals, or in patterns of interactions (a distinction referred to as the power of conceptualizing the problem)?
2. Does the therapist take a stance outside or, perhaps, above the family requesting help, or does the therapist see himself or herself as joining a circular process (the order of embeddedness of the knowledge required)?
3. Does the therapist behave as an expert who dictates a solution or as a facilitator of conditions of change for the family (the level of solution attempted)?

From a cybernetic perspective, help on the organizational level is to consist of the latter category of each of these three distinctions (Krippendorff & Steier, 1979). This kind of help is referred to as a morphocatalytic approach.

Historically, most therapists have conceptualized problems as systemic (distinction 1). Fewer have seen themselves as joining a circular process (distinction 2) or as facilitators of change (distinction 3). As Hoffman (1981) noted, however, many views of family therapy have recently shifted to theories of intervention that encompass a view of therapists as both joining a circular process and as facilitators of change. In fact, family therapy is in the vanguard of the helping professions in this regard. While family therapy has made this leap, research on the efficacy of family therapy has not. Research on family therapy continues to proceed as though families are clinical objects on which an intervention is performed, as though families are passive systems that produce an output (outcome) when given an input (therapy).

Varela (1984) spoke of a paradigmatic shift that is occurring through cybernetic theory. He described it as a shift from an input/output (or, Turing) systems paradigm to an autonomous systems paradigm. Using as a metaphor a cocktail party at which each guest participates in multiple conversations simultaneously, Varela emphasized the necessity of seeing the multiple interconnections and reciprocal relations that characterize a system. These interconnections, taken together in the form of organizational patterns, generate the coherence of a system. These organizational patterns can be seen as constructed wholly within the system; it is to this closed loop of organizational relations that the concept of autonomy refers. (This concept of organization refers specifically to the set of invariant relations by which a system constitutes itself, i.e., those relations that are necessary for a system to maintain its identity [Maturana, 1970].)

In order to understand the autonomy of a system (including the observer), it is necessary to understand the way in which it is organizationally closed. This is a paradigmatic shift that emphasizes the circularity of internal transactions, but does not ignore the system's context. For example, Varela (1984) mentioned the importance of understanding the way in which the system is structurally linked to an environment, that is, the way in which the system's varying set of relationships change in concert with its environment. This understanding is precisely what researchers should be striving for when they study change that co-occurs with family therapy.

Varela (1984) developed these ideas with specific reference to biological systems, in which the relations of interest are those of production (such as the self-production of cells). The relations that specify the autonomy of a social system, such as a family, and its identity are relations of communication, stipulated through language. That is, the types of relations that define the family system are constructed in a social domain (Steier, 1985).

The focus on the family as an autonomous system allows both the therapist and the researcher to consider a family and how it changes in a different way. This new approach involves a much closer examination of the relationships which make up the family, the internal reciprocity of those relationships, all in the terms of each particular family. This is the researcher counterpart to the therapist as facilitator. Family therapists as facilitators of change do not steer families to a "best" model of a healthy family, but recognize the variety of forms that healthy families might take, or even the variety of organizational relations that healthy families use to construct their concept of family (Jorgenson, 1983; Jorgenson & Steier, 1984). A similar approach may enable researchers on the effectiveness of family therapy to improve the basis of an entire research program on the meaning of family change.

Instead of trying to see how a group of families change on a common set of measures, for example, researchers should consider the relevance of that group of measures for each family according to a family's self-description and the observer's description of that family. The measurement of the same variables may *mean* different things for different families. For example, two families may have the same "score" for some measure of enmeshment, but the extent to which enmeshment is a prominent descriptor of each family may be quite different. Families are not different seeds in the same field; they exist in different fields.

In short, an autonomous systems view leads researchers to ask different questions, to consider therapy as a perturbation with a family system and to study the family's co-occurring compensations. This is not a mere shift in terms, as the perturbation-compensation approach allows the family therapy researcher to focus on internally generated changes within the family. This perspective calls for the inclusion of methods of a more ethnographic nature in the study of family therapy effectiveness. Although traditional statistical design methods need not be abandoned, it should be understood that such methods are based on

assumptions that guide how outcome is created. An ethnographic approach provides more information on the changes that are taking place in the family's own terms and, as such, provides a better basis for future large-scale programs, when they are appropriate (Agar, 1980). Family therapy efficacy research has jumped too quickly to address the question of "which is better" without really considering what "better" really means. Rather than seeing the variations in therapeutic systems as something that needs to be "controlled" for, we need to study precisely that variation.

RESEARCH PROGRAM AS AN OBSERVING (AUTONOMOUS) SYSTEM

The traditional emphasis on control of variation, while well suited to the kinds of questions for which such statistical designs were intended, does not always fit the change process often met in family therapy situations. The procedures that were so useful to Fisher (1951) in his desire to answer agricultural questions of differing crop yield under differing conditions and motivated its experimental design can inhibit the questions that must be addressed in family therapy research. The dilemma is a methodological determinism (Monge, Farace, Eisenberg, White, & Williams, 1984); the effect that traditional design methods and traditional research questions have on each other puts constraints on both.

If one is comparing a family therapy intervention to, for example, a non-family treatment, one of course wants to be able to specify exactly what the family therapy entails. It is in this sense that at least some uniformity of the characteristics of the family therapy are needed. However, specifying in advance exactly what these characteristics are, at the level of therapy practice, is an attempt to control a natural feedback loop.

A family therapy program is a circular system that involves interconnections between many people, including families, therapists, researchers, and supervisors. Relationships that connect the various participants create the coherence of the program. Communication between, for example, therapists and researchers permits the natural evolution of the family interventions over the course of the entire research program. Thus, information about what changes in previous family systems were facilitated by which therapeutic techniques reverberates throughout the research program as a system. Data about the way in which interventions change are to be included in an assessment of the efficacy research program, that is, the processes by which data are generated are themselves data of interest.

In order to understand fully the efficacy of family therapy, it is necessary to understand the larger system, the research program, in which the family therapy is embedded. This requires a family therapy program to include an understanding of itself, as an autonomous system, characterized by its own circular internal interconnections. By means of participant observation, for example, members of a family therapy program can see themselves as an observing system, responsible for an understanding of all program processes. Any intervention program, such as one involving family therapy, should be a self-reflexive entity.

SOME THEORY-BASED RECOMMENDATIONS

1. Participants in therapy research programs must be aware of the process of how the presenting problem gets recursively constructed between clinical interviewer, client, and context.

2. Since family therapy is based on systemic change, and not just on removal of a symptom, family therapy research must include systemic change, not as an adjunct to removal of the symptom, but as outcome itself.

3. The family therapy researcher must see variations in family organization not as something just to be controlled, but as data that contribute to an understanding of the therapeutic process and allow research to focus on internally generated changes within the family.

CONCLUSION

The model of family therapy research as a process of self-reflexive interpretation is parallel to a "hermeneutic circle," which presents research as a "merging of horizons" of the researcher and "other" (Salmond, 1982). It blurs the traditional distinction between a therapist as one who performs an intervention and a researcher as one who "objectively" evaluates that intervention. Good interveners are always researchers in the sense that they create their therapy in part by reflecting on which interventions were successful and which were not. Researchers may also be interveners, as the very act of asking a family questions admits the possibility of changing the perspective and/or behavior of that family. Perhaps it is the recognition of the blurring of the researcher-intervener distinction that lies behind the power of therapy such as the Milan approach (Selvini Palazzoli, Boscolo, Cecchin, & Prata, 1980) and its variations (Penn, 1982; Tomm, 1984).

Too often, issues in family therapy research programs are labeled "therapy issues" or "research issues" and are considered of interest to only a part of the staff. Family therapists have been struggling for years against an approach that sees problems as parts of a system, rather than in the interactions that make up the whole. Family therapy researchers must be able to see themselves in the larger system of interactions in which they exist.

REFERENCES

Agar, M. (1980). *The professional stranger: An informal introduction to ethnography*. New York: Academic Press.

Ashby, W.R. (1956). *An introduction to cybernetics*. London: Chapman and Hall.

Bateson, G., Jackson, D.D., Haley, J., & Weakland, J. (1956). Toward a theory of schizophrenia. *Behavioral Science, 1*, 251–264.

Dewey, J., & Bentley, A. (1949). *Knowing and the known*. Boston: Beacon Press.

Fisher, L. (1982). Transactional theories but individual assessment: A frequent discrepancy in family research. *Family Process, 21*, 313–320.

Fisher, R.A. (1951). *The design of experiments* (6th ed.). New York: Hafner.

Frankel, R.M. (1985, March). *Discourse and text: Social construction of clinical reality*. Paper presented at Temple University Department of Speech Sixth Annual Conference on Discourse Analysis. Philadelphia.

Hoffman, L. (1981). *Foundations of family therapy: A conceptual framework for systems change*. New York: Basic Books.

Jorgenson, J. (1983). *Conceptions of family: A communications approach*. A proposal for research. Annenberg School of Communications, University of Pennsylvania, Philadelphia.

Jorgenson, J., & Steier, F. (1984). *The family's construction of a concept of family: The organizational dimension*. Unpublished manuscript.

Krippendorff, K., & Steier, F. (1979). Cybernetic properties of helping: The organizational level. In R.F. Ericson (Ed.), *Improving the human condition: Quality and stability in social systems. Proceedings of the Society for General Systems Research Silver Anniversary International Meeting*. London: Springer.

Kuhn, T.S. (1962). *The structure of scientific revolutions*. Chicago: University of Chicago Press.

Maturana, H.R. (1970). Neurophysiology of cognition. In P.L. Garvin (Ed.), *Cognition: A multiple view*. New York: Spartan Books.

Maturana, H.R. (1978). Biology of language: The epistemology of reality. In G.A. Miller & E. Lenneberg (Eds.), *Psychology and biology of language and thought: Essays in honor of Eric Lenneberg*. New York: Academic Press.

Monge, P.R., Farace, R.V., Eisenberg, E.M., White, L.L., & Williams, K.I. (1984). The process of studying process in organizational communication. *Journal of Communication, 34*, 22–43.

Morgan, G. (1983a). Research strategies: Modes of engagement. In G. Morgan (Ed.), *Beyond method: Strategies for social research*. Beverly Hills, CA: Sage.

Morgan, G. (1983b). Exploring choice: Reframing the process of evaluation. In G. Morgan (Ed.), *Beyond method: Strategies for social research*. Beverly Hills, CA: Sage.

Penn, P. (1982). Circular questioning. *Family Process, 21*.

Salmond, A. (1982). Theoretical landscapes: On cross-cultural conceptions of knowledge. In D. Parkin (Ed.), *Semantic anthropology*. New York: Academic Press.

Selvini Palazzoli, M., Boscolo, L., Cecchin, G., & Prata, G. (1980). Hypothesizing-circularity-neutrality: Three guidelines for the conductor of the session. *Family Process, 19*.

Stanton, M.D., Todd, T.C., Heard, D.B., Kirschner, S., Kleiman, J.I., Mowatt, D.T., Riley, P., Scott, S.M., & van Deusen, J.M. (1978). Heroin addiction as a family phenomenon: A new conceptual model. *American Journal of Drug and Alcohol Abuse, 5*, 125–150.

Steier, F. (1985). *Reflections on a meeting/Scenes from a courtship: Cybernetics and family therapy.* Unpublished manuscript.

Todd, T.C., & Stanton, M.D. (1983). Research on marital and family therapy: Answers, issues, and recommendations for the future. In B.B. Wolman & G. Stricker (Eds.), *Handbook of family and marital therapy.* New York: Plenum.

Tomm, K. (1984, November 2). *Circular interviewing.* Presentation given at annual meeting, American Society for Cybernetics, Philadelphia.

Varela, F. (1984, November 1). *The cybernetics of autonomy.* Address given at annual meeting, American Society for Cybernetics, Philadelphia.

von Foerster, H. (1979). Cybernetics of cybernetics. In K. Krippendorff (Ed.), *Communication and control in society.* New York: Gordon and Breach.

von Foerster, H. (1981). *Observing systems.* Seaside, CA: Intersystems.

von Glasersfeld, E. (1984). An introduction to radical *constructivism.* In P. Watzlawick (Ed.), *The invented reality.* New York: Norton.

Watzlawick, P., Weakland, J.H., & Fisch, R. (1974). *Change: Principles of problem formulation and problem resolution.* New York: Norton.

Wiener, N. (1948). *Cybernetics: Or control and communication in the animal and the machine.* Cambridge, MA: M.I.T. Press.

4

The Cybernetics of Family Therapy and Family Therapy Research

David Kantor, Ph.D.
Kantor Family Institute
Cambridge, Massachusetts
and
The Family Center
Somerville, Massachusetts
and
Lucille L. Andreozzi, Ed.D.
Research Associate
The Family Center
Somerville, Massachusetts

A T THE FAMILY CENTER IN Somerville, Massachusetts, cybernetic principles are being used to study the relationship of process to outcome in family therapy. In the spirit of Wiener (1967), who suggested that "organization is the message," and other cybernetically oriented epistemologists who emphasize form over matter and pattern over substance (i.e., substantive findings in this instance), the researchers in this project are investigating organized patterns of the family therapy process as they relate to an overall understanding of practice and outcome. Accordingly, the research was designed with two interrelated purposes in mind: (1) a redefinition of the use(s) of research and the functions of the researcher, using cybernetic perspectives and terminology; and (2) the application of a model in which the researcher is viewed and utilized as a component in the information feedback system.

Unlike traditional approaches to research in which efforts are made to maintain scientific objectivity, the research strategy at the Family Center is intended to have a positive effect on therapy. Furthermore, therapy is not seen as something that stands apart from its subject (i.e., families, family therapist, change, and process), nor as an isolated or isolatable entity. Instead, it is viewed as an interactive process set in motion by the systematic interrelations of several co-influencing elements—namely, the family, the therapist, the therapist's method, the supervisor, and the components of the administrative process that bear significantly on clinical operations (including, in this instance, the research operations themselves).

At the Center, service and research are considered two interdependent components of a single, unifying treatment mandate: to develop a program that maximizes service capabilities. Each component has a degree of autonomy, and each is constrained by the other in a relationship of reciprocal responsibility that is governed both by operational realities and by official policy. Thus, the Center's stated policy on service is to identify areas of acute human need and to respond to such needs by developing and implementing treatment models that are routinely subjected to critical assessment and change. The Center's stated policy on research is to develop a research model that not only is valuable in critically assessing the Center's treatment activities, but also, by openly contributing to an understanding of the concepts that underlie these activities, is both affected by and responsive to Center operations.

CYBERNETICS AND ITS APPLICATION TO FAMILY THERAPY

In a position paper issued by the American Society for Cybernetics, von Glasersfeld (1983) described the impact of cybernetics. Reflecting on the wide ranging impacts of the approach, he described cybernetics as "metadisciplinary," rather than "interdisciplinary," in that it "distills and clarifies notions and conceptual patterns that open new pathways of understanding in a great many areas of experience" (p. 3).

Cybernetics has had numerous applications, both technologically and conceptually, since its inception 35 years ago. Technological applica-

tions have included automatic pilots, industrial robots, and the most obvious symbolic representation, the computer. In the field of management and political science, cybernetics has been successfully applied in systems for understanding human relations, the relationships of things (e.g., parts to wholes), and patterned development of roles. Additional applications of cybernetic theory in philosophy, logic, mathematics, cognitive adaptation, the biology of cognition, and physics, as well as world relations, are all shedding new light on every cybernetician's focal concept—the phenomenon of self-reference.

In the present application of cybernetics at the Family Center, attempts to effect positive therapy outcome are promoted through an ongoing, self-conscious understanding of the conditions under which such gains occur. The influence of the concept of self-reference is widespread, but it is most noted in the *way* treatment programs are organized and in the epistemological implications of our research tools, methods, and instruments.

TREATMENT IMPLICATIONS

Underlying all program development at the Family Center is the proposition that any attempt to influence others is ultimately self-referential. In traditional treatment approaches, most manifestations of self-reference (e.g., countertransference in psychoanalytic therapy or nonneutrality in systemic family therapy) are viewed as problematic, if not as a breach of good clinical form. In the cybernetic understanding of clinical realities, however, self-referential operations are regarded as inescapably integral to the feedback loop known as the therapy process.

Two concepts, boundary profile and formed versus forming structures, have been introduced as a dramatic means of formally managing self-referential phenomena in therapy. These concepts have been paired with two other clinical concepts at this point in the research, namely, the therapist's model and method. All four concepts, or more exactly the manifestations of these operations as they appear and are noted within the therapy process, are studied both for their pattern of influence and for their overall effect.

Boundary Profile

A therapist's boundary profile is the more or less discrete set of organized tendencies that govern his or her relations in intimate worlds, including the therapy world. The boundary profile has two frankly deterministic components, both representing functions of self-referential operations in the therapy process: (1) perception(s) and (2) activities or behavior(s). The therapist has a tendency to perceive individual and family structures according to categories derived from personal past experiences in key relationship structures. Similarly, the therapist tends to behave in characteristic ways or patterns when encountering those client characteristics that most resemble or reawaken key foundation experiences and relationship structures from the therapist's own past. A specific set of internalizations, or critical identity images (Kantor, 1980, 1983, in press; Kantor & Neal, 1985), imbue as well as account for the majority of such tendencies to perceive and to act in predictable ways within specific contexts. In the interactional field of therapy, such tendencies inevitably lead to the evolution of what are called forming structures.

Formed versus Forming Structures

Formed structures are derived from the therapist's theoretical perspective, from what the therapist is prepared, on theoretical grounds, to "see" in a dysfunctional family system. In the same family, one therapist sees "disturbed boundaries"; another, "faulty communication"; another, "triangulations"; still another, "disturbed hierarchies." Forming structures, in contrast, evolve in the course of therapy from the therapist's (often unarticulated) personal explanatory system and construction of reality. When the therapist is no less immersed than is the client in the therapist-client interaction, these emerging structures often remain unnoticed and unattended by therapist and researcher alike; however, these structures are frequently known to clients.

Because structures actively mediate between the therapist and his or her therapy techniques, they often have more bearing on therapeutic outcome, both positive and negative, than do the therapist's more readily observable formal interventions. Therefore, any attempt to understand more fully the mutual, reciprocal relationship of process and outcome (i.e., of therapeutic process to differential outcome) must inevitably and systematically address these phenomena. To ignore such phenomena as they emerge and unfold in treatment is to proceed blindly through the therapy process at great expense to both client and therapist.

Therapist's Model versus Therapist's Method

Companions to the fundamental principle of self-reference are the concepts of self-regulation and self-organization. These two concepts converge in the Center's heavy emphasis on the development of clinical models (i.e., models of therapists, supervisors, researchers, and the Center itself). Models are differentiated from methods in the Center's training, supervision, and treatment programs, where a clear distinction is drawn immediately between the "method" (e.g., structural, strategic, systemic, transgenerational) that a therapist elects to use in a given case and the clinical "model" that the therapist is actually *evolving*, both across cases and over time as he or she continues to develop and change.

A therapist's method is an already formalized, theoretically organized clinical perspective. It is a particular way of seeing a system's disabled structures and may involve a specific plan for intervening that includes recommended techniques and strategies for staging change. A therapist's method is usually associated either with a specific family therapist/theorist or family therapy group.

A therapist's model includes not only one or more theoretical perspectives, but also the therapist's boundary profile, personal explanatory system, model of the ideal family, and the self-corrective mechanisms that are available to the therapist in interacting with particular families in treatment. It is assumed that the therapist's model, the family's model, and the model implicit in the therapist's elected method are interdependent, compromising a feedback loop whenever a therapist is providing treatment.

A therapist's model is largely implicit; however, it has a significant effect on the therapy process and outcome, and all therapists at the Center are asked to make their models explicit. Because a therapist's model is not a finished commodity, but rather is an evolutionary process that develops throughout a professional lifetime, Center therapists are expected only to state what they know and do not know about their model's status and functioning in clinical contexts and to assume responsibility for these operations. By encouraging therapists to distinguish between supposed or assumed clinical realities, often synonymous with method, and the actual clinical reality found in the model, we have discovered a wide range of new and different treatment structures for study and description.

Integration of Cybernetic Principles into Routine Practice

At the Family Center, we are attempting to formalize and regulate self-referential concepts by integrating them into routine treatment operations. Thus, for example, features of the therapist's boundary profile that are likely to be potentiated in a given case are included in the official folder for that case, and their possible effects on both the diagnostic and treatment process are monitored by the therapist, supervisor, and researcher. Information about the workings of boundary profile and forming structure phenomena is obtained through specific items that appear on the Rainbow Forms, the set of family therapy process-outcome forms in use at the Center.

In the Center's overall concept of the therapeutic process, the relationships between observer and observed, between client and therapist, between supervisor and supervisee, between clinical environment and supervisory staff, and between research and therapy are seen as "mutually dependent couples" (term adapted from Maturana, 1980). Because aspects of outcome are thus formulated in terms of "couples" that interact to create a combined reality, outcome is never viewed as entirely objective. On the contrary, all clinical outcomes are judged and treated as shared constructions of reality. Therefore, in the Center's model, no component or "couple" is left to its own devices, but is challenged to document its model. Each component system must distinguish between its own model of reality and that of all other respective component parts.

USE OF RESEARCH BIASES

The research model of reality naturally contains within it a concept of effective therapy. If our research has biases, as all research does, they can be found in the strong position taken on how successful therapy is conducted or, more generally, what comprises the basics of any successful therapy. When these biases are made explicit, they pose fewer "threats" to the validity of the study's findings.

Treatment Plans

The Center's position on treatment plans is threefold:

1. Treatments that lack a plan tend to drift.
2. Every preconceived treatment plan is a presumption of certainty.

3. Any therapeutic plan that smacks of certainty is presumptuous and pre-emptive of client realities.

From this perspective, complete certainty about the best way to help others change is viewed as a patent absurdity. Nonetheless, we acknowledge the value of making presumptions and certainties known in the clinical process, since we think they exist; simultaneously, we acknowledge the value of qualifying these presumptions and certainties under the constraints of the clients' equally compelling presumptions and certainties about how to change.

This position, openly proclaimed as a research bias, is conveyed to trainees and staff by supervisors who, when they themselves do not endorse such a position, are asked to announce their own bias. The intuitionist, explorer, or discoverer therapist or supervisor may argue, for example, that planners (especially invariable planners) fail to understand the true nature of the therapy process or the role of the therapist in it. Consistent with the Center's multireality stance, a researcher at the Center may respond that any nonplan is in actuality a plan. Such an explorer therapist or supervisor at the Center is asked only to take responsibility for his or her model, however, not to alter it.

Items on the Rainbow Forms have been designed to elicit information on planning. The forms include assessment items, such as

- Do you have a definite plan?
- If yes, to what extent does it borrow from the type of plan associated with your method of choice?
- How certain are you that your plan will work?

- Who in the family is likely to show most resistance to your plan?

Following such assessment items, items that call attention to potential, boundary profile activities may appear on the forms:

- Are your feelings toward the supposed resister familiar to you from past experience?
- To what extent does your therapy plan reflect your personal views about how to solve life problems?
- What is it about this family that contributes to your certainty or uncertainty about whether your therapeutic plan will work?

Also included on the forms are items that suggest the therapist's need for help such as "If you have no plan for this family at this time, check which of the following statements apply: (1) I prefer to work without a treatment plan. (2) I need more time to discover a plan. (3) I am confused and need help."

The Staging of Change

In some therapy approaches, the staging of change is central; in others, implicit; in still others, not to be found at all. The Center's position on this issue, a position that trainees can challenge but not replace, is quite specific: the staging of change is one of the most important keys to efficient therapy. Items on the Rainbow Forms clearly address this issue, eliciting therapists' views about how they deal with this therapy process dimension in their practice. Therapists are asked, for example

- Does your method of choice include a stage theory?
- If yes, are you familiar with it?

- If yes, do you plan on using it?
- If no, do you see this as (1) irrelevant, (2) a problem you want help with, or (3) of no consequence at all?

Therapy Forecasts

The therapist's estimation of the amount of time it will probably take to reach the designated therapy goals is a forecast. Some therapies are explicit about the prescribed length of time. For example, brief strategic therapy calls for 8 to 10 sessions (e.g., the Mental Research Institute (MRI) group); other therapies suggest that therapy should be brief, but do not specify a specific time period; and still others, whether they address this specific issue or not, imply that therapy may take time. In order to ensure that therapists consider the length of time that the treatment of specific cases may require, the Rainbow Forms contain such items as "How long will it take to reach your therapy goals?" and "Who in the family is likely to agree or disagree?" Raising such issues via the research instrument items not only calls the therapist's attention to the theoretical function of time factors inherent in different family therapy approaches and theories of change, but also sets the stage for an even more fundamental issue. It draws therapists' attention to the way in which the interfacing of the family's model, the therapy model, and the therapist's personal theory often alters the "official reported method" to produce, in contrast perhaps to what is described in final case summaries, the actual "model" that unfolds in the therapy process.

DEVELOPMENT, DESCRIPTION, AND OVERVIEW OF THE INSTRUMENTS

The research at the Family Center is organized around an overall objective: to develop instruments for documenting the contribution of the family, the therapist, and the supervisor to therapy process and outcome. To date, however, the research has focused primarily on one variable in the therapy process-outcome relationship—characteristics of the treatment method, including some initial attention to the interactive, evolving co-influence of therapist on method(s) and method(s) on therapist. The instruments used to document this component of therapy process are comprised of six color-coded Rainbow Forms: Blue, White, Green I, Beige, Yellow, Green II, and Pink. Each form represents a different aspect or vantage point on the therapy process.

The Rainbow Forms contain three general types of items—sensor, assessment, and flag items or signals to therapists—each with an important feedback function. Sensor items sensitize the therapist to factors in the therapy process, especially those introduced and/or generated by the therapist, that ordinarily remain unnoticed or, if detected, unattended (e.g., aspects of the therapist's boundary profile that may interfere with or alter therapeutic process). Assessment items focus on the therapist's facilities for comparison and critical self-evaluation. Flag items encourage the therapist to "yell for help," acknowledging the therapist's professional and personal vulnerability and, therefore, increasing his or her awareness of reciprocal involvements in the therapy process. All three feedback functions and the items that represent these functions help the therapist develop the power to make informed discriminations about events in the therapy process.

The Rainbow Forms are not intended to remain static or fixed. Because there are no fears about "contamination" in this research model, the research instruments, no less than clients and therapists, are subject to change and influence. In fact, the evolution of these forms over time provides its own kind of descriptive commentary and critical feedback account of the co-influences of research on therapy and therapy on research. Therefore, via the reported impact and use(s) of the forms by therapists, the forms as well as the form items are revised.

Occasionally, the research team, in order to "make a point" (i.e., a systems intervention and statement), deliberately does not alter items declared troublesome by therapists and/or supervisors. Here, the team's "resistance to change" carries a message, perhaps that the trouble is not with the forms but with the supervisor's teaching capabilities or with the line therapist's ability to comprehend the concepts being taught. Such an occurrence provides an opportunity for dialogue among all concerned parties. As a matter of Center policy, there is regular interaction between researchers and clinicians; this process itself can be mutually beneficial. Over time, as a function of such dialogues, the Rainbow Forms and form items have tended to become simpler in format, while simultaneously reflecting more complex aspects of the therapy process. In sum, the forms encourage self-regulative over hierarchical operations.

The Blue Form and Its Clinical Uses

The Blue Form, the first of the Rainbow Forms to be completed, charts the therapist's assessment of a client system.

On this form, the therapist answers questions about the "problem" from multiple, concurrent vantage points (e.g., the perspectives of the family, the referral source, and the therapist). These questions tend to legitimize the notion that there are often different perspectives among various people and contexts on many system levels (e.g., between family members as well as between the treatment agency and the referral source).

One major cluster of items on this form is designed specifically to help the therapist select an appropriate method of treatment for the particular family. In developing this cluster, the researchers encountered several difficulties. The primary dilemma facing them resided in the points of distinction noted among major family therapy theories and family therapies. The fact that the family therapy theorists whose methods provide the treatment and, therefore, the diagnostic frameworks for Center staff "see" disabled family structure differently weighed heavily in the design of this form. In keeping with our convictions about the legitimacy of multiple realities, we are self-mandated either to eliminate or to reveal the bias of our own theoretical perspective in the construction of the questions.

Our temporary solution to this dilemma has taken several forms. One is the use of generic language in posing questions to therapists, such as "Identify the power structure in this family. Who is in charge? Who makes decisions?" Another is the use of language associated with a particular treatment perspective, such as "Rate the degree of closeness (enmeshment) and distance (detachment) between family members." A third is the introduction (in some sensible sequence) of a major concept associated with each of the major family therapy schools. The construction of the form is thus a statement in itself. It encourages therapists to make informed decisions as to the proper match between the particular family in treatment and their own professional orientation or method of choice.

In a course of therapy whenever a therapist gathers and uses new diagnostic information, he or she is encouraged to complete a supplementary Blue Form. From the supervisor's perspective, the appearance of none, some, several, or many Blue Forms spliced between the clusters of other forms is an immediate color-coded indicator that "something" is taking place between the client and the therapist in connection with the assessment or diagnostic process. To one supervisor, the appearance of many Blue Forms may suggest "drifting" or "unfocused therapy"; to another supervisor, the presence of numerous Blue Forms may seem quite appropriate. The process of reviewing the form goes beyond the differential meanings and clinical interpretations that various supervisors ascribe to the presence of some, none, or many Blue Forms, however; it requires supervisors to reflect on their own therapy and supervisor model and to distinguish between these and the therapist's method and model.

The White Form and Its Clinical Uses

The information contained in the Blue Form is distilled on the White Form, which resembles a traditional case summary. The White Form serves two basic purposes: case presentations in supervision and responses to requests for information from other treatment agencies. The form is a consolidated descriptive case summary, culminating in a systems diagnosis and a systemic hypothesis that specifically identifies the therapist's views on what structures need change and the projected appearance of these structures following therapy.

In contrast to those on other Rainbow Forms, items on the White Form do not have (with one exception) built-in sensor, assessment, or flag messages. This one exception involves the form's last item—the systems diagnosis map. In designing such a "map," the therapist is asked to use his or her theoretical orientation and chosen method to conceptualize the client system in spatial terms and to diagram the structures that he or she proposes for change. The message conveyed in this task is simply that, if the theory is systems oriented, then the structures that it identifies can be represented in relationship terms.

This systems mapping carries both educative and clinical messages. The item requires therapists to conceptualize the structure proposed for change and to think about the import of their predictions. It forces the articulation of an important issue underlying all therapy process and outcome—whether the therapist's chosen method proposes an ideal for healthy family functioning. Furthermore, therapists must determine whether the proposed after-treatment structure represents their own or their theory's model. These questions help therapists to test their theories and methods, and to organize and formulate their working therapeutic processes. Most therapists do operate with a desired outcome structure as a guide, but few ask what is the cost of having one, not having

one, or having one that is discrepant with their personal model or that of the client family.

The White Form requires therapists to make one other distinction in examining the change process. Therapists are directed to "specify," in units from 1 to 10, the amount of change for each element (e.g., child, parent, couple system) represented in the before-and-after system maps. This item helps to make therapists aware that their model for change may contain within it rather specific statements on how, for instance, mothers, fathers, spouses, and children are "supposed to be" in relation to one another and that their own bias against one or another or these system components may be implicitly operating.

In requesting therapists' quantification of estimated change, the research, once again, is playing it "both ways." Looking outward, it reminds therapists that any evaluation of change that fails on some level either to quantify or to standardize between-method measurements is dealing in estimates so gross and/or subjective that comparisons across studies and therapy approaches are meaningless. Looking inward, it suggests that these quantifications are not to be taken too seriously; they represent analogues of biases and the judgments that therapists are always making (although they are often unaware of the impact of such judgments on practice). By quantifying these judgments on the White Form, therapists may develop a greater sense of responsibility for such clinical estimations and, ultimately, outcome decisions.

The Green I Form and Its Clinical Uses

The Green I Form, which must be filled out "no later than the fourth session," represents a kind of declaration of therapeutic intent. With the exception of those therapists in specific training programs, therapists do not as a rule put their treatment plans and forecasts in writing. On this form, however, therapists are asked to do so if they can (again, the question itself reveals its message value to the therapist). Therapists know that their declarations on the Green I Form are not indelibly cast in stone, however, since there are ample provisions for revising a plan if information obtained in treatment suggests that it would be appropriate to expand or change original hypotheses. Therefore, the more tentative therapists proceed with less trepidation.

The Beige Form and Its Clinical Uses

The Beige Form documents the therapy process. It poses those questions that any good supervisor would ask a therapist: "Did you have a plan for the session? Did you follow it? What techniques did you plan? What techniques did you actually use? Did they work? What did you focus on? Have you formulated any new hypotheses? Is change taking place? What next?" This form also poses questions that few supervisors would ask, unless they had been alerted to a problem by some revelation during a supervisory session. These questions include "Did you feel powerful? In charge? Was your family experience *in* the session today? Who did you like/dislike, feel close to/distant from, unsexy/sexy toward? Did anything happen to let you know that you have some growing up to do?" Through the routine repetition of supervisor-like questions, each designed to give as well as to get information, items on the Beige

Form encourage self-supervision (self-regulation) in the therapist. By dividing and, therefore, alternating references to the therapist with references to the technology (i.e., therapy method), this research form and format clearly and unmistakably shows that the therapist and technology invariably interact.

The final three items on the Beige Form, comprised of two sensor items and one flag item, are designed to elicit and heighten the therapist's awareness of the influence of his or her boundary profile, including possible effects on and involvements in forming structures. Collectively, these items invite therapists who detect boundary profile issues in specific family therapy cases to ask for help and/or clarification from appropriate sources (e.g., supervisors, other therapists, self-reflection on the forms).

The Yellow Form and Its Clinical Uses

Completed after every fourth therapy session, the Yellow Form is designed as a review of the events and progress of therapy. It challenges therapists to crystallize their clinical formulations and to assess, integrate, and explain to others and themselves their therapy machinations. The Yellow Form, in short, asks the therapist to be accountable. In completing this form, therapists are asked to put their method not only on the table, but also on the line.

Before the session, the therapist is expected to address such questions as "What structures do you expect to be working on today? Where do you want to intervene? What techniques do you expect to use?" After the session, the therapist faces "What is the relationship between the structure you actually worked on today and your diagnostic map (the structure you have identified for change)? Have any changes taken place, positive or negative? What 'stage' of therapy are you in? Do you have a stage theory of your own? How long will it take you to complete this stage? What systemic orientation are you using? Are your techniques appropriate?''

Like all the Rainbow Forms, the Yellow Form is designed to refocus the therapist toward the client family context; it reminds the therapist continually to consider such questions as ''Given this family's form of disablement, is your orientation appropriate? Given this family's paradigm or model of reality, as you know it, is your approach appropriate?'' Going a step further, the form items extend to an examination and exploration of the therapist and his or her method through such probes as ''From what therapeutic stance are you operating? Given your understanding of your boundary profile, are you mismatched with this family? If yes, explain how, if you can. Is your therapeutic stance appropriate? Is your method appropriate?''

Items on the Yellow Form, first having directed the therapist's reflective gaze retrospectively to the beginning phases of therapy, then deeply settling the therapist's attention within the here and now of the present case, finally prepare the therapist for the transitional phase and the eventual termination process. In sum, the Yellow Form may best be described as manifesting a type of relentless quality or ''circular questioning.'' It helps therapists determine whether their method is working to their satisfaction.

The Green II Form and Its Clinical Uses

Currently on the researchers' drawing board, the Green II Form is being designed for three main purposes: (1) to condense, summarize, and integrate otherwise discrete elements of information on the therapy process into relationship statements or descriptions in context; (2) to highlight and depict visually the larger patterns of influence and response that underlie all phases of the therapy process; and, by accomplishing both of these initial objectives, (3) to provide therapists and supervisors with ready tools for the self-monitoring and evaluation processes. More specifically, this form is intended to depict graphically the relationship between the therapist's overall treatment plan and his or her session-by-session method.

In order to produce the Green II Form, the researcher codes the information reported on the Green I Form (therapist's treatment plan) and the Yellow Form (therapist's method and progress); a computer then transforms the coded information into a graphic representation of both the progress and the pattern of ongoing therapy. For instance, each computer printout is a Green Bar representation of the results of the coded data. In the near future, a series of graphic overlays will be superimposed on the Green Bar coded summary information in order to provide therapists and supervisors with a self-contained, flexible ''read-out'' on the therapy process tracked from multiple vantage points and on various process levels.

The Green II Form will indicate (1) how well the therapist's theoretical model (i.e., combination of reported data on therapist's method and plan) is working throughout different phases of therapy and/or therapy sessions; (2) whether the therapist is "on," "ahead of," or "behind" schedule and by how much; and (3) the type and direction of the relationship between the therapist's model and the therapist's method as it unfolds in therapy. One other important future use of the Green II Form will be to indicate "therapy ingredients" that seem to cut across all the major schools of family therapy. For example, when therapists' reports of the treatment of similar cases by means of different therapy methods are examined, do common ingredients appear across successful outcomes? Are therapists from different professional orientations doing similar things?

The Pink Form and Its Clinical Uses

The Pink Form focuses on the final phase of therapy, the termination process. Most family therapy orientations pay little attention to termination issues, but we at the Family Center believe that (1) the termination process should be addressed on some level, (2) the level of attention should correspond to the given therapy method's stance on this issue, and (3) the termination process should reflect the type of family served and the type of presenting problem. For example, an intact family with a difficult adolescent may respond readily to brief therapy, which may end abruptly; however, a multiproblem family with such problems as abuse or incest will ordinarily require more extended family therapy.

The Pink Form's focus, as is the case with all the Rainbow Forms, is cybernetic. Its items call attention to the inter-

relationships among therapist, client, and method. The form poses questions to the therapist such as "Given your treatment method, did the therapy end as you expected? Were you surprised? In what way(s)? Describe the sequence. Who initiated termination? What did you contribute to the way in which therapy ended? What did your method contribute to the way in which therapy ended? What did the client contribute to termination? Whether you are, or are not, satisfied with the way therapy ended, did your way of ending affect the process? How?"

INTERACTION OF PRACTICE AND RESEARCH

The color-coded nature of the forms provides immediate information about the therapy process, quite apart from their content. For example, a qualified person who picked up a case folder that contained eight Yellow Forms (review and assessment), each one interspersed not only with the anticipated three Beige Forms (therapy process), but also with a sprinkling of five Blue Forms (diagnostic process) and three White Forms (diagnostic map), each of the latter followed by a Green I Form (therapeutic plan), would know without reading a word that the therapist is conducting an extended therapy (8 × 3 or 24 sessions) with this case and that the therapist has added new diagnostic information from time to time, resulting periodically in changes in the therapeutic focus and treatment plans. In such a pattern, certain critical questions arise that can be readily answered by turning to single items in the forms, all easily accessed.

Before each session, supervisors review supervisees' most recent forms. Prior to the biannual evaluations that therapists receive from their supervisors and supervision group, therapists review all case folders, formulating their own analyses of patterns in their treatments within and across cases.

The number, depth, and range of questions that can be posed and readily answered is constrained only by the knowledge and imagination of the trainee, therapist, or supervisor. Moreover, when the forms do not answer a question that seems significant, the questioner may suggest to the researcher that one of the forms be revised.

PROGRESS ON INSTRUMENTATION

All six therapy process forms are currently in use, in various stages of development. In addition, efforts are under way to develop instruments for obtaining family data, both from the therapist's perspective and from the family's perspective. Feedback *from* family *to* therapist and researcher, under conditions not entirely controlled by therapists, may be the most unattended feature of therapy process research. If differential therapy outcome is to be understood and if various interested publics are to gain confidence in the researcher's efforts to conduct meaningful assessments of therapy process and outcome, however, the families must be seriously considered, both for their organizationally varied natures and for their contributions to therapy process and outcome. To date, it is rare in the clinical and research literature to find families differentiated except according

to descriptive and/or demographic characteristics. Rarer still are accounts or commentaries on therapy in the words of clients, reflecting their own unique perspectives.

Finally, attempts are under way to gather information on the interactional effects of therapists' characteristics in therapy process and outcome. Under development is an instrument that we hope will identify the therapist's personal theories of family dysfunction and family change. These may be major variables that, along with the therapist's boundary profile, mediate between the therapist and the theoretical model and method that he or she is using in a given case. As for the therapist's boundary profile, items that refer to it are included in each of the six therapy process forms, and a draft of a therapist boundary profile chart has been roughly completed. Beginning when the therapist is a trainee and/or novice therapist and continuing throughout his or her professional lifetime, the therapist gradually fills in the chart's "cells." Peers and supervisors, from their observations of the therapist's activities, help fill in the chart and share responsibility for it with the therapist through designed feedback. These forms constitute, for the time being, our attempts to instrumentalize therapist characteristics that may be operating in the therapy process.

Ultimately, instruments will be developed for investigating all five major sets of variables (i.e., therapist, method, client, supervisor, and setting) and the contributions each makes to therapy process and outcome. In this research model, instrumentation and instrument use serve a two-fold purpose. They are a means for gathering information that can be descriptively summarized and/or analyzed with clinical, research, or administrative goals in mind. By virtue of the special construction of the instruments and the care with which they are being institutionalized at the Center, however, they also constitute a mechanism for change in and of themselves.

REFERENCES

Kantor, D. (1980). Critical identity image: A concept linking individual, couple, and family development. In J.K. Pearce & L.J. Friedman (Eds.), *Family therapy: Combining psychodynamic and family system approaches.* New York: Grune & Stratton.

Kantor, D. (1983). The structural-analytic approach to the treatment of family developmental crisis. In J.C. Hansen (Ed.), *Family therapy collections: Vol. 7. Family life cycle* (pp. 12–34). Rockville, MD: Aspen Systems Corporation.

Kantor, D. (in press). Couples therapy, crisis induction, and change. In A.S. Gurman (Ed.), *Casebook of marital therapy.* New York: Guilford Press.

Kantor, D. & Neal, J. (1985). Integrative shifts for the theory and practice of family systems therapy. *Family Process, 24,* 13–30.

Maturana, H.R. (1980). Biology of cognition. In H.R. Maturana & F.J. Varela (Eds.), *Autopoiesis and cognition.* Boston: Reidel (original work published in 1970).

von Glasersfeld, E. (1983). *Declaration of the American Society of Cybernetics.* The American Society of Cybernetics.

Wiener, N. (1967). *The human use of human beings.* New York: Avon.

5

'Circularity' in the Management of a Case

David Kantor, Ph.D.
Kantor Family Institute
Cambridge, Massachusetts
and
The Family Center
Somerville, Massachusetts

T HE FOLLOWING THERAPY process account does not conform to the usual case presentation. Instead, process data on outcome have been organized to depict outcome from a variety of concurrent treatment system vantage points (e.g., supervisor, therapist) and from multiple family system levels (e.g., family, parental, marital, sibling, symptomatic child). In order to convey the multidimensional nature and simultaneity of interaction within the family therapy process, the individual participants' accounts have been combined and integrated. Information was derived from three main sources: (1) actual in-session interaction; (2) the present family context, both in and out of therapy; and (3) flashbacks or past associations in which experiences in the past converge with relations in the present, both in and out of therapy.

Moreover, unlike other case presentations, this case account includes certain individuals who are known by most practitioners to affect the therapy process and the management of a case directly and/or indirectly, but who are seldom cited as ''participants.'' Those directly involved in the case include Jim, the father, and Celia, the mother, from the Halpern family; and John Sayer, therapist trainee, and Anne Peretz, supervisor, from the Family Center staff. Those indirectly involved in the case include the three Halpern children, Rachael (aged 13), Andrea (aged 12), and Jamie (aged 8), and Alan Slobodnick, supervisor, from the Family Center staff; Betty Farbman, administrator, and David Kantor, director of research and training, from the Family Center, other members of the research team; and the research itself.

All the participants played a crucial role in the management of the case and in the way in which the therapy process eventually unfolded. Their case accounts capture glimpses of ''outcome'' and ''circularity of relations'' rarely alluded to, if not completely overlooked, in usual case presentation formats and most family therapy outcome studies.

THE HALPERN FAMILY—A BRIEF INTRODUCTION

The Halpern family was self-referred. In a telephone interview, Jim explained that he and his wife Celia (aged 38 and 36, respectively) wanted help with a problem that their 8-year-old son, Jamie, was having, both at home and at school. About 1 month before the telephone call for therapy, Jim reported that Jamie had begun to have nightmares, was performing significantly below level at school, and had started clinging to his father, especially on weekends. Jim also described a change in Jamie's mood. Jamie had become listless and showed signs of social withdrawal, a symptom that Celia called ''depression.'' The two Halpern daughters, Rachael and Andrea (aged 13 and 12, respectively), were ''not implicated,'' although Celia felt that they were ''acting up'' and should be included in therapy. Jim agreed.

THE WIFE'S POINT OF VIEW

''Celia is tough,'' Celia thought, calling forth her habit of addressing herself in the third person in order to keep a proper perspective (even within the recesses of her innermost thoughts). ''Tough,'' she thought, ''but not tough-minded. No, dammit, not tough-minded.'' If only Jim could ''get it,'' just get the distinction, their problems would be over. She knew she still loved him, but her will to ''hang in there'' was weakening.

Her toughness was *not* closed-mindedness, as Jim insisted. She simply ''wanted more'' from their marriage, and she hated (yes, it shocked him) his ''plasticity.'' Jim seemed to have no mind of his own. His deference, even his kindness, seemed to sicken her. Plasticity . . . even at the peak of his rage—picturing him at the not so awesome height of about one foot and a half, Celia laughed to herself, simultaneously criticizing her own cruelty. After all, he was given to saying, ''Celia, you made your bed [yes, she had cut him off], but I don't have to lie in it.'' When therapy started, she was sleeping in the family room on the pull-out couch. She was not angry, just resolved—deliberately pulled back into herself and her convictions.

Yet, in her usual way, she was open with the kids. ''Too open,'' Jim had complained. ''It's just a difference in styles,'' she argued. ''It's not as if we're getting a divorce.'' Gathering the children together around her one evening after dinner, she had informed them (''maybe a little too matter-of-factly,'' Jim later said) that she and Jim were having a fight. His critical stance on the way she told the children about their ''fight'' titillated her more than he could imagine or know. ''If he would only fight back. . . .'' The rearoused love juices fading fast, she mused about how they loved their kids in different ways, instead of about how she once loved him.

Yes, she enjoyed cuddling the children as much as he did, but Jim failed to discriminate. He loved them both when they were obedient and when they committed infractions against the family's altogether too lenient rules. He loved their son and two daughters *equally,* at all times, without discrimination. Now how the hell could that be? "How in Goddamn hell could that be," her father's words surfaced in her. "They were his words," she thought, first smiling, then frowning, as her memory of her father and her mixed emotions about strengths and weaknesses coalesced into an image at once known and lost to her. No, she was not against cuddling and coddling. Like her father, however, she discriminated between "occasions" and "just rewards." "If love isn't unconditional, then it isn't love," Jim would argue on those rare occasions when he did argue. "But earned love is sweeter," Celia would retort, immediately silencing him, a form of victory that depressed her.

Jim had become annoyed, not exactly argumentative or angry, but at least annoyed when she had let the children know why she was sleeping on the family room pull-out couch. To his credit, she thought, that show of annoyance or converted version of anger had led them to seek help.

A stream of thoughts began to trickle through the cracks of Celia's resistance; her power to discriminate "occasions" from "rewards" did fail sometimes in Jamie's case. Jamie,

their youngest, was her favorite. She knew that. He could do no wrong. Jamie's birth had taught her what bonding really meant, an intimate deep feeling of attachment and protection, even satisfaction. She had to feign anger when the girls' complaints about Jamie were justified, when he had, in fact, done something wrong. "Cruelty is not your only vice, Celia," she reminded herself. "Even worse, there is your selective dishonesty that stands out at times like some speck of grease on an otherwise well-tailored dinner napkin," she admonished herself. "Well, who says consistency ever was my maiden name," she countered, partly from righteous indignation, partly in defense of herself. Then, not exactly putting these meddlesome thoughts completely out of her mind, she returned her thoughts to the decision to seek therapy, a decision made the night she told the kids that she would probably be sleeping in the family room for a while.

The kids' reactions bothered her the most. Their reactions were like an unexpected slap in the face. Rachael's quick response, "Does that mean we can't watch TV early Saturday morning?" and Andrea's smart rejoinder, "Yeah, we get up earlier than you on Saturdays." Jamie's unshakable silence or "silent statement" hurt her the most, however. Celia remembered explaining all this to John Sayer, their therapist, in the first therapy session.

She had tried and was still trying to tell it all as honestly as she could to Jim and the therapist, without shoving the truth down the kids' throats.

What she had neglected to share in therapy, but did finally, was that Jamie's silent statement struck a blow to what she had thought was her own private reality. When she told the kids that she would be sleeping in the family room for a while, her 8-year-old Jamie stood there, one hand shielding his eyes, the other hand inside his pajama bottoms touching his genitals. "Christ! And I thought psychoanalysis was dead. If that wasn't a telegraphic statement about Jim and me, what is?" she said to John in the therapy.

John, she thought at the time, was too young to handle the stickier nuances of her relationship with Jim, but did seem competent enough to help with the kids. He seemed to have a positive effect on the girls' blank wall of indifference and on Jamie's nighttime terrors, daytime depression, and declining performance at school. He seemed, in an ironic kind of way, to treat the problems without treating them. While distrusting his indirectness (a loving, manipulative way of getting things done just like her mother's), Celia simultaneously felt grateful for its palliative effects on the kids.

She had trouble with John and his "therapy" in the way he handled her, Jim, and their relationship, however. There, he seemed cavalier and one-sided. She understood his game; she was smart. She just forthrightly refused to play it his way. For instance, she knew he wanted to "upgrade" Jim, and that, after all, was her aim, too. For her own selfish sense of well-being, she knew she needed a more solid, less plastic man ("Yes, Celia, someone like your father")—not a man who was like clay to be molded any which way, but one who would argue back and, by taking a stand, show he cared. Even if she succeeded alone in "solidifying" Jim's weak neutrality, however, it would be she who was shaping Jim and Jim who was being shaped. So she knew she needed and wanted John's help; but she also knew that John, like her father, had gone *too far*. She could tell he needed "to win." In truth, she could not quite tell at this point whether he had a thing about winning at women's expense. She liked his sense of direction, and she thought he liked that quality in her, too, at least at first. Yet, when she began to pick on Jim in one session, partly because she was piqued at something Jim had actually said, partly as a conscious plea for help from John, an opportunity to give him a chance to equalize things, John went too far . . .

"Look, Celia," she cautioned, "something in him seems to enjoy a bit too much any opportunity to put the woman down and raise the man's status. But even worse, poor dear, he seems deaf, dumb, and blind, Celia, to the clues you've been dropping like bread crumbs all over the place. Instead of taking responsibility for his own mess, he played with you and your resentments, staying on top even with playing at being one-down." It was the truth of this claim that led Celia to bolt from therapy. Surely, she had seen *it* happen, not once or twice, but several times in the 10 or 12 sessions. She now had to contend with two unacceptable men—one, unmovable, the other, all too easily moved. Utterly exasperated, what else could Celia do but leave the men to each other and their own devices?

THE THERAPIST'S POINT OF VIEW

In some respects, John preferred the old way of being supervised. All he had to do to look good was to figure out the supervisor's game, check the rules in his *Manual of Personal Experience with People in Authority Positions*, and play by those rules. By following this dictum, he had made it through graduate school with honors. Now, he was doing it again at the Kantor Family Institute and the Family Center. John did not especially like the part of himself that knows how to survive in these ways, but he was, he knew, a survivor.

With Kantor, the real power around here for John, surviving was easy. Humor him (and he feels loved), then tell him that you are humoring him (and he respects you). With Kantor, the sure way to a secure and nearly equal position of power is by judiciously commandeering your way through the unobstructed domains of affect and meaning. Take him on in the mine-filled obstacle course he calls the domain of power, however, and watch out. Although he does not know how he appears to people (just a little bit smarter than he is), one thing you can say about the bastard is that he lives his own theory.

Dealing with Anne, the supervisor, is a different matter. Oppose her quickly and forthrightly, let her score her power points; but only when you're sure she's right. To play to power or to humor her

gets you some short-term, but no long-term access to her overly large but not always certain heart. Once you have a foothold, take a straight path to her missionary garden, the fortress of her very being.

While John was confident of this assessment, he also knew that his supervision sessions had not gone so well of late. In fact, he could pin the downward turn to Anne's announcement that "from here on, we'll be using the Rainbow Forms (Kantor & Andreozzi, 1985) in supervision"—John was no longer so sure of the rules. Reviewing the most recent session, he felt somewhat shattered, but *informed* (one of Kantor's favorite words). Anne had asked him to bring the case folder on the Halpern family to the session. A new rule. Then, she skipped very quickly over the chitchat. Another new rule. Whereas David (John's didactic supervisor) rarely bothered, the preliminaries with Anne (his case management supervisor) were important; John could always gauge the 'points' he would score in a supervision session by the quality of those first 5 or 10 minutes of chatty openers.

Like a third party on a date, the Rainbow Forms came between them, cooling things. The forms sat loosely in a pile as Anne flipped through them, passing the Beige Forms, but stopping to scan item #2 on the Yellow Forms.

"You're pretty faithful in filling these out. Like them?"

"No, but I find them useful."

"You skipped only one Yellow Form; otherwise, they're all here."

"I vaguely remember being pressed that week." He recalled now that feeling unexpectedly defensive, he had privately recited David's proclamation:

"The Rainbow Forms are part of the therapy research loop. You are not punished for not doing them or rewarded for doing them. Those are bureaucratic strategies. The mandate to 'use them or not' is a systemic strategy. If you fail to use them, only ask yourself, what information does that decision give you?"

"Did anything *special* happen in the session you skipped?"

"Not that I recall." When Anne then handed him the two Beige Forms that should have sandwiched the missing Yellow Form, John instinctively glanced at his responses to items #7 through #12.

In the earlier session, he had marked all 9s and 10s on item #7, which meant that he felt "satisfied with his efforts," "powerful," "in charge," and "able to follow a carefully planned strategy." Item #8 showed that he focused on Mrs. Halpern in the session; item #9, that he "felt stuck but managed to avoid an impasse;" item #10, that something did "happen in the session that reminded him of a person or experience in his own family," but that he did not "use this awareness"; items #11 and #12, that he "felt particularly close to Mr. Halpern" and "distant from Mrs. Halpern until I got by the near impasse, thereafter, feeling close to her as well." John compared his responses on these items. Lighting up with a bit of self-recognition, John observed, "The joke is on me. It seems I didn't get beyond the impasse."

As vividly as if it were happening now, John recalled Celia's exit at the end of the session. He saw her rise, even shoot upward from her seat, and almost run toward the door. He saw Jim scurrying after her, trying to erase the distance between them and to cover up the fact,

only now realized by John, that Celia was not leaving a session, but was bolting from therapy. Sans farewell. Understanding it all suddenly, John decided to remain silent. Something in the way Anne's glance returned to the form told him she knew and did not need to say anything. "Should we look at the other Beige Form?" Anne invited after a pause. To her credit, John had thought, she made a very decent effort not to seem triumphant. "No thanks!" John responded rather quickly, with an element of defensiveness that he could not hide.

John instantly put some diverse pieces of clinical and self-information together. When Celia failed to appear for the next session, he redefined the unit of treatment and the structure that he was addressing in the therapy. Or, rather, Celia's absence had resulted in a new definition of the treatment unit and structure.

In another painful flashback, John's next almost involuntary recall felt like a slap, reminiscent of a blow delivered by his sister in a fight they had when he was 9 and she was 11. Approaching the waiting room where Jim sat, the kids wrapped around him like fox furs, he noticed that Celia was absent. "Celia couldn't come today," Jim had said, blushing. "She said you had speculated that we needed some time to work on my relationship with the kids and that you might want to take advantage of her absence." "Bested by the bitch," John remembered mumbling under his breath. By the time he had climbed the stairs, the Halperns trailing behind, and entered the treatment room, he had appropriated Celia's plan as his own and felt relieved. I'll have to redo item #9 on the Yellow

Form (the pre-session plan), he thought. He knew, however, that he had not done that.

If the decision to redefine the treatment unit had been primarily or principally John's decision, the rationale for the shift would undoubtedly have appeared in item #2 on the Yellow Form. Had he completed the Yellow Form, he would have had to justify this shift; examine the relationship between the structure he had initially identified for change on the diagnostic form at the end of the assessment process; and, since there was indeed a discrepancy, either reconsider his decision to shift focus or revise the diagnostic form accordingly.

He did none of this, he knew. He never even completed the Yellow Form, the "stop and consider" form that is usually completed on every fourth session. In a sense, he had not even noticed until now how pivotal the session had been. "Amazing," he said to Anne as he put these pieces together, "amazing how that happens, this knowing but not knowing, this 'not noticing.'" Starting to notice, his head was exploding with fragments of information—about his mother and sister, and the sinister pleasure he felt when managing to best them at cards, in intellectual arguments, and in their attempts to keep his father off balance in what he came to call "the family's gender politics."

Anne, John concluded, had made a brilliant move when he alluded to these family matters after the information flooded his mind: "In my supervision model," she said, "it would be appropriate for me to hang out with you on these matters. The subject matter is delicious. I see isomorphisms at every interface . . . you and your family, you and

your client family, you and me. If I follow my model and dig in, on one level I can't lose. After all, I'm the boss, I'm the supervisor. On another level, I can't win, nor can you. To use the power inherent in this relationship would not serve me well at this point. It would be cheating if I did. Instead of indulging my predilections, why don't we each take whatever information we can glean from what this is telling us and do our own work on our own. Instead of my trying to teach you something by redressing the balance of gender power in the politics of this case, let's simply look together at the computer print-outs. Help me find those 'patterns' that David and the research team say we can find. You're better at this stuff than I am. It's still largely a jungle to me."

"Cheating!" Her words rang loud. "It would be cheating . . . ," she said. Well, he knew about that. Winning, through the clever manipulation of power, always felt like cheating to him; but, he confessed, he enjoyed it. As a little kid, it gave him an erection. No, he was not ready to put this into the boundary profile jacket of the Halpern case folder. For now, he would enjoin himself to be especially vigilant in future contacts with Celia and rethink his therapy plan. He had a great deal of sorting out to do there. Surely, he was caught up in one of David's "forming structures." He thought he had won, but he had not and had even failed to notice that he had not. He was "cheating" and would have to back up with Celia.

In order to avoid cheating with Anne, he must not only take her up on her invitation to look at the computer print-out together, but also do so without exploiting the one advantage that he had over her. It was true that he knew better than she did how to look for patterns on computer print-outs. He also knew better than she what David meant when he said, "The power of any information the forms give amounts to nothing if it is not self-referential": the mere looking for patterns is as important as the findings. From Anne's not very subtle skepticism about the forms in past sessions, John knew that she had not caught the essence of David's message.

The rest of the supervision session went well for John, although he had to feel his way through a fog that periodically settled in whenever something reminded him of his power game or its impact on the therapy. (The self-referential process at work, he thought, each time it happened.) He especially liked helping Anne understand the full implications that his clinical faux pas had on his therapy with the Halperns.

He had not bothered to examine the print-outs before. Doing the Rainbow Forms was enough, he thought. The print-outs were merely coded extrapolations of the therapy process. Besides, Anne had never referred to them or brought them to supervision sessions before. So, he had never seen the Green Bar Column. David was not yet satisfied with them. Although Anne tried her best to represent fairly David's enthusiastic claims that examination of the Yellow and Green Bars could reveal at a glance the relationship between a therapist's method and model, John knew that she was as skeptical as he was. He and Anne had both been audience to David's sometimes rabid mutterings: "Of all the distinctions the research asks you to make, none is more important than the distinction between therapist's method and model." The reason that this was so

monumental escaped John, nor had he fully grasped what the distinction was.

When he and Anne examined the two columns in the Halpern case computer print-outs, John was proud. "By the way," Anne had begun, "this is only one of three print-outs that has Green Bar data. Of the Family Center's 16 interns, only you and 2 others have been sufficiently clear about your 'models' to warrant coding by the research team." Responding to John's unuttered thought, Anne had added, "Yes, only 3. I thought it was terrible, but David was delighted. 'Now we know more about what they know and do not know,' he said."

With this, John's mood took a cautious turn. ("I prefer 'knowing' to 'knowing what I don't know,' " he thought. His pride beginning to fade, John inspected the Yellow and Green Columns with Anne. She said, "This dotted line across the Green Bar represents how far the therapy should have gotten, that is, according to your method's prediction. It comes, I think, from a couple of sources, your Yellow Forms mainly. This solid line represents how far the therapy has come. It falls short of the dotted line."

John's mood swelled again, this time with anger. "I feel tricked . . . criticized . . . ," he muttered. "If I'd had these print-outs from week to week, I'd have done something about the discrepancy." Had he hesitated only a moment longer, these words would never have spilled out. He anticipated Anne's reply by a split second: "Precisely," they chorused. They laughed. He got it.

THE SUPERVISOR'S POINT OF VIEW

In a supervision session earlier in the week, Anne had felt dissatisfied somehow with John, the way his work seemed to be going, and her own supervisory performance. Later, she would recall that in the peer group session that she and other supervisors attend, she had lied when she was asked, "Do you like this trainee?", a question that was becoming routine in the new format being used at the Center.

Unfolding the computer print-out, a summary sheet of the entire therapy process conducted to date by John, she held it at arm's length, in part to erase her instinctive resistance both to research and computer technology. She had hated the whole business when David first introduced the idea of computer-assisted therapy and supervision. "Research that gives as well as gets information," David kept saying, "research instruments that are integral to the cybernetic loop we call therapy . . . research whose product is not objective truth but increased wisdom and responsibility." She could and did fight him, tooth and nail, but he had the power to insist that she, like the other supervisors, try it.

Lazily, she counted the unfolded sheets, three 8½ × 11 pages. Knowing that each sheet contained information on 8 therapy sessions, the three sheets meant that the client family had been seen in more than 16 sessions but no more than 24. Noting the third sheet showed information only in three columns, Anne instantly calculated that John had conducted 19 sessions with the family. Some questions began absently to form. "A lot? Too many? Enough for this family?" As an experienced therapist and supervisor, Anne knew that the answers to such questions are relatively complex; however—and here at least she is willing to give David some

credit for his "cybernetic" hogwash—she does have a place to go for some perspective.

Anne ran her eyes across the print-out. Her mind recited, "Green bars appear following every 4th therapy session. They represent the therapist's model, or *what he knows of it*. It functions primarily as the therapist's check on himself." (David's voice piggy-backs on her thoughts, adding his emphasis.) Glancing back to the last green bar, the last column on the second print-out sheet, dated a month before, she read "16/8/15." Noting her pride in understanding what all this means, she was embarrassed, but decoded, "This means that on the date at the head of the column, John conducted his 16th session; that in the model he decided to use with this family, he predicted that he would have accomplished what he has currently accomplished by the 8th (not the 16th) session; and that he expected to reach his therapeutic goals in the 15-session therapy series.

Anne knew that, in her own preferred therapeutic model for treating this family, a 30-session series would not be out of the question. In the rhythms of her own inner map, John was on schedule. In the rhythms of his model, however, he was very much behind. Grudgingly, Anne conceded another point to David and his confounded Rainbow Forms. Before being pressured into using them, she more than likely would have helped John to "see" the family the way she does and to design the "proper" course of therapy from her theoretical and clinical perspective. "Verboten!" David had shrieked. "He should no more take over your model than you should mine. By inflicting your model on him, as most supervisors do when working under conventional training formats, you would be impeding learning.'' In truth, Anne was given at those times to reflecting that supervisors are hired for distinction, for expertise. Trainees are taught by straight, direct instruction, by modeling, by gentle direction along the right path, the path already known to the supervisor. ''You can present your model,'' David argued, ''but only as an alternative perspective. The trainee can borrow it, or parts of it, but unless you inform him of the consequences of that choice in the event he's making a bad epistemological match, again, you are delaying his learning. The task is to teach the trainee to develop a model of his own. Let me ask you a question: When nobody is looking, when you are doing therapy that is not for teaching or demonstration purposes, do you, most of the time, do what you were trained to do?''

Anne did not like the question or her unspoken responses, but she did not like his answer either. It seemed so ungraspable, so out of step with everything she had been taught, so steeped in impossible ambiguity. Although free-wheeling on one level, Anne was also concrete. ''Tell me anything. But tell me.''

As Anne turned back to the print-outs of John's therapy sessions, she remembered how the support of Betty Farbman, the Center's administrative director, for the Rainbow Forms as ''one of the few disciplined things going on in this place'' helped tip the balance in her, Anne's, hold-out with David. Although Anne never took back her testy ''prove their worth'' stance, Betty's support of the forms gave a lift to her tenuous conviction that the forms might be useful. She had to admit that the forms provided a

more solid ground of concrete information. She scanned the top lines of the form. John had begun by seeing the whole family; switched in session 9 to seeing the couple; and scheduled his 12th meeting also with the couple; but instead the man came with the kids. He then scheduled to see the couple for two more sessions, taking them to the 14th, thereafter scheduling both parents and the children, with the mother missing every alternate session until the 19th.

Anne had many critical thoughts about John's treatment patterns. She does not like John. ''That's irrelevant,'' she thought, admonishing herself. She heard David's rejoinder, uttered so many times on so many issues, ''Be careful to ask the right question of the data. You're critical, I would guess, either because he touches off a structure in your boundary profile, or because your treatment model is different from his. Your critical attitude, as well as your self-admonishment, are a reflection of your asking the wrong question.''

Anne's thoughts came to an abrupt halt. ''There's that damn concept again: boundary profile! [boundary profile: roughly, a tendency to form in therapy or supervision certain kinds of structures when interacting with specific structures manifested by the client system].'' Anne initially had loved the concept. After all, she agreed with David's pronouncement that therapists are inescapably part of the therapy equation and that the issue should be addressed at the Center. ''But in this so-called research, is he not going too far?'' thought Anne. ''Surely he is when he insists that the therapist's boundary profile should be included in the case folder of every client he or she is seeing in therapy and that the outcome of therapy should not be assessed if the therapist is excluded from the loop. He even goes so far as to intimate that in assessing change we ought not to look only at change in clients, but change in the nature of the loop that includes client and therapist. Fine in principle; in reality, a potential disaster.'' She remembered asking David whether the staff would be honest.

''It doesn't matter, so long as the research forms remind them that they are not.''

''Won't therapists use the opportunity to pay more attention to themselves than to their clients?''

''That is only terrible if they never get to know that about themselves. Perhaps we will have to revise the forms again.''

''If we do include the therapist's boundary profile information in the case folders, will we agree to reveal this material to outsiders, Blue Shield or other third party payers, for example?''

''If we decide knowingly to withhold such information from those we do not trust because we doubt they can use the information, we are at least being responsible to ourselves.''

''Is the field of family therapy ready to take on the question of accountability?''

''What matters is that the right questions get raised.''

Her thoughts returning to John and to the case she is attempting to supervise, Anne grudgingly conceded that the Rainbow Forms were making her think differently about therapy, supervision, and the running of a treatment center. Having touched even lightly on those of her boundary profile features that appeared to be operating in the supervisor-supervisee loop, she felt freer to pose other ''right questions.'' Anne asked herself,

''Does John have a clear therapy model? Is he following it? If he's revised either his model or his diagnosis, has he used the forms to note this? Has he lost sight of the structure he originally set out to treat? Are his plans from session to session consistent with this model? Does his model provide for the staging of change? Does he have any idea how to select the appropriate techniques for bringing about his desired change in the different stages? Have features of his boundary profile contributed to the creation of forming structures that are interfering with his attempts to alter the already impaired formed structures? Has he called for help, and/or have his calls for help escaped you, either because you were not using the forms as an aid in supervision or because you couldn't use them because you are involved with him in an evolving forming structure that is interfering with your effective use of your own supervisory model? Do you have such a model?''

In considering these questions, Anne remembered another conversation with David in which he had said, ''A clinical model specifies regularities in the changes between input, the therapeutic interventions that are associated with the method the therapist has elected to use, and output, the desired modifications in client behavior.''

''Does a therapist need a model?''

''Without one, it is like performing surgery in the dark.''

''Do all therapists have one?''

''Yes, but therapists are notoriously lazy. They keep it hidden, even from themselves.''

''Must we be so hard on the poor therapist?''

"Actually, the problem is not with therapists, but with training programs and practice settings. They do not ask therapists to pay attention either to the problem of formulating their models or to the necessity of becoming conscious of the process."

"Aren't you forever condemning programs that emphasize or teach a particular method?"

"A method is not a model. You can teach a method; you can't teach a model. A model is a particular therapist's application of the particular method or methods he is using in the particular case, at a particular point in time."

"You haven't addressed my question. Why do you condemn programs that emphasize a particular method?"

"Because they often mislead the very therapist or trainee whom they wish to instruct."

"By . . . ?"

"By failing to distinguish between method and methods, between a method and a model, and by failing to instill in therapists the responsibility for knowing about the evolutionary nature of their own particular models."

"But why condemn? These distinctions require such refinement of thought. Do they matter?"

"A great deal. They spell the difference between health and malaise, both for therapists and their clients."

"Those are big claims, David. I sure hope you are clear about the criteria for realizing each of these outcomes. They appear to depend on whether the therapist's method(s) match his model and whether the therapist's model matches the client's. Are you arguing against mismatches? If you are, you're in trouble with those family therapists who

claim that disruption of a family's paradigm is essential to change. Aren't they in effect saying that when they disrupt they are unraveling a client's model or construction of reality through confrontation with their own."

"The problem isn't whether there is a match or mismatch, but whether the therapist allows that a match or mismatch in models of reality may be desirable for change to come about in a particular case."

"The therapist is responsible for that, too?"

"Most assuredly!"

"For discovering the circumstances for successful outcome of therapy?"

"Most assuredly!"

"I see. Through an awareness that each person's model of reality is valid and through taking responsibility for deciding when a match or a mismatch between his own and the client's models is appropriate?"

"Indeed."

"You realize, of course, that you are nudging the therapist's responsibility into the realm of morality."

"That's where it belongs, ultimately."

"You are also defining the therapist as a researcher."

"Yes, especially those therapists who are willing to pay attention to how they and their models operate in the information (i.e., "influence") exchange loop."

"Interesting."

"Do you see, Anne, why we need to build this particular research into the Family Center's operations and that it, too, must be looked at as a model that plays a part in the loop?"

"It's a bit boggling. All these realities—the client's, the therapist's, that of his method, the supervisor's, and now that of the research. Boggling. My head's going around in circles. . . . "

Anne paused for a moment, temporarily disengaging herself from these perplexing circular thoughts. Returning her thoughts to the Halpern case, she scanned the computer print-out before her. Checking the Green Bars, every fifth column on the computer print-out, Anne determined that John apparently did have a clear clinical model. A 15-session therapeutic plan had been mapped out after the third session. From the looks of it, his model was based on a modified brief strategic therapy approach. To check this assumption, Anne examined the primary Blue Form, a detailed diagnostic form that is completed early in therapy and documents the therapist's diagnostic thought process. On item #16, John had checked "strategic therapy" as the preferred therapy method for this family.

On a hunch, Anne flipped to the back jacket of the case folder where John's boundary profile information was kept. She learned from scanning his responses on 50 scale items that John rated historical and transgenerational approaches high, and brief therapy approaches low. "That's curious," she mused, "John's personal therapies for changing families are much like my own." Anne observed first a softening of her feelings toward her trainee and then the warning—"As a supervisor, your job is to help your supervisee develop his or her own therapy model, unless your supervisory model calls for training all trainees in your clinical likeness, in which case you must take some responsibility for the consequences of that decision. Does it? Do you have a supervisory model? If you

do, are you using it in a self-conscious way, visible to others?" By this, David had meant, was she using the Rainbow Forms to document her own supervisory process?

"Well, I am not . . . too much damn effort on top of everything else." Anne could imagine David's reply: "If not, you run the same risk of therapeutic failure as does any supervisee who does therapy without a model for bringing about the desired changes. If not, if you are supervising without a model, you must keep yourself as much apart from the therapy loop as you can, forewarned that you cannot possibly succeed anyway. By failing to develop your own training model and failing to take advantage of some external reminder (such as our research forms) that helps you to remain aware of your own operations, you will influence supervisory and therapy outcome in some unknown ways. Your best bet, then, would be to direct your supervisee back to the therapist–Rainbow Forms–client loop, which is my preferred model for supervising, but doesn't have to be yours, provided. . . ."

Anne found herself rehearsing her next challenge to David: "Am I to conclude that John as a therapist and I as his supervisor are not to have direct influence over the change processes in which we are engaged?" Too soon and not without resentment, she anticipated David's answer: "We should be concerned not with direct influence but with indirect influence, remembering that it is impossible to check either completely. Placing our emphasis on the observer's (therapist's, supervisor's) own operations means placing emphasis on the therapist's awareness of the self as a limited, yet one of the most powerful, humble, and high-reaching sources of wisdom there is.''

Anne laughed to herself, recalling the reaction of Alan Slobodnick, another supervisor, when David answered the question "What, concretely, is the primary goal of this research; what is the point of these forms?" by saying "An increase of wisdom and responsibility in the therapist.''

"Where does change in the client system come into play?''

"If the first happens, the second will also.''

"What is the relationship between this wisdom you speak about and knowledge of techniques and the staging of change, which occupy such an important place in our teaching?''

"Wisdom is knowing how to use such knowledge.''

Anne knew that Alan was not yet using the forms in his therapy and was using them only perfunctorily in his supervision. Anne then remembered citing for David instances in which trainees had told her that they, too, were completing the forms perfunctorily, or, worse, not completing them consistently. "I'm worried, aren't you?'' she said.

"No.''

"What are the right questions?''

"Are students consistently skipping certain items? Does this mean that they cannot answer those questions? Are we therefore mistakenly thinking that, because we "teach them" in seminars or supervision sessions how to recognize system structures, they can recognize these on the clinical firing line? Do they even know what they don't know? Is the very existence of the forms instrumental in alerting them to what they are doing

and what they don't know about what they are doing? Are we asking ourselves similar questions, based on the trainees' responses on the forms? After all, these are the true purposes of the research forms, to give such information.''

"But, still, why are you not worried?''

"Supervisees cannot possibly get full value from the forms unless the supervisors are convinced of their value and begin to use them.''

Anne turned her attention back to John's forms and to the computer printout that summarized his 19-session, not yet complete therapy series with the Halperns. She remained ill at ease with the Rainbow Forms. Until now, she had used them sporadically. When she tried her best to use them, she felt ignorant. She thought, "I do better when I solve imponderables by crashing into them headlong and putting my opposition out into the open. Now that's the most obvious feature of my boundary profile. It occurs to me that something about John's arrogance resembles David's . . . resembles . . . . '' With that thought, she made a mental commitment to start working formally on her boundary profile and began to enter the print-out jungle in the hope of finding answers, or better questions.

THE HUSBAND'S POST-THERAPY POINT OF VIEW

His back to the recently tucked-in Jamie, Jim Halpern hesitated at his son's bedroom door. He was held frozen by a fleeting glance from Celia, who was sitting with a book in the living room across the hall, shadows of colored light from the fireplace calling attention to what Jim called her "cynical eye." Such fleeting glances could "turn him cold."

He had learned a great deal from John, the family therapist, and from the therapy, now over by 5 months. Celia had, too, although not nearly as much as he. Even she acknowledged it. "He never made it with me after his faux pas," she had confessed. Most to benefit were the kids, Jim surmised, as he turned first left toward the family room, then right toward the study. He chose the cozy back corner of the hall the Halperns sardonically called "the study" to write a long-neglected letter to his father in Philadelphia, seeking privacy there because the girls were in the family room watching TV and doing their homework. "Not true," he thought. He chose the cozy corner because the pull-out couch was pulled out.

But, yes, the kids benefited a great deal. Like their mother, the girls were less enthusiastic about the therapy. Unlike their mother, however, they had learned to like John, his secret pleasure at one-upmanship turning them on as much as it turned their mother off. After Celia had angrily confronted him on this tendency (when she returned after refusing to attend a few times), John had at first seemed ready for intellectual confrontation, a brawl. Jim remembered with a feeling of disloyalty how he had inwardly looked forward to the battle and Celia's defeat. John did an abrupt about-face, however; excusing himself, he called his supervisor, Anne, and returned a few minutes later, altered in mood. "My supervisor is of the view that you, Celia, are right to protest. Jim, she believes, doesn't protest enough, either with you, with the kids, or with me. Your [Celia's] modeling of self-assertion,

though it has resulted in some difficulty in your marriage and though it has caused you personal pain, is for a good cause in this family."

This clever move, Jim realized, deflated Celia's anger in the session, allowing other things to happen. The girls took issue with their mother and with the mysterious Anne. The precocious Rachael said, "Don't make this into a feminist war, Mom. This has nothing to do with men and women. It is about the right to express differences." Jim was proud of his 13-year-old daughter, but remained silent. He hated taking sides. John, in continuing, played it both ways. Reinforcing Celia's protest, he complimented the kids on being free to challenge their mother, as well as Jim and Celia for creating a climate in which this was possible. "Individuation," he had called it, or was it "differentiation?" Jim forgot which. Even Jamie, who seemed to respond more to the prevailing mood and people's feelings toward one another than to the words they used, seemed to get something out of it.

This had been the turning point in the therapy, Jim thought. The whole family was invited back for a few sessions, although Celia managed to find last minute reasons for not attending—in Jim's private opinion, just for spite. She said that the kids were benefiting, even if she was not. "So let them be the focus. That's why we came, isn't it?" As for her, the therapy had reached its limits. She could not trust John to help with the marriage. Jim could tell John how she felt if he chose, or if Jim wanted, she would tell John what she thought. But that was that.

Sitting at his desk to begin the letter to his father, Jim reflected that Jamie's troubles seemed long past. Celia was no longer on Jim's case about his "sickening libertarianism." She even pulled back from Jamie a little, leaving the field to Jim without the ever so subtle obstructions that she used to raise. Hats off to Celia, he thought. None of this had been dealt with in the therapy, nor had it even been openly dealt with between him and Celia. Somehow, something had been resolved for Celia, and in this area, at least she was now uncritical of him.

Not so in matters of sex. Jim wondered about his "inbred reticence to confront nasty issues," as Celia put it. When Celia took the telephone call that was a post-therapy follow-up interview for the Center, she told Jim she had given a positive report on the family's progress; but, she added with a trace of sarcasm unmasking her deliberate matter of factness, she had said that Jim might want to call later because his view might be different. This, Jim knew, was an invitation for him to complain about the state of their sexual affairs. Jim had declined, however, and never made the call. Although suspicious of his own decision to remain silent, he had concluded that, for now, silence was the better part of valor.

Recently, Jim reflected, Celia too had drifted into silence. Three weeks ago, the last time he had seen her openly angry, she had said that she would go for couples therapy if he wanted to, but not with John Sayer. (In that discussion, as in so many throughout their married life, Celia's flair for nuance both perplexed and exhausted him. Strange, since that was what attracted him to her in the first place.) That she would consider "that Anne woman" puzzled him. Celia hated the telephone intervention, which she attributed in part to Anne. "It grabbed me like three pairs of hands pulling me in three directions at once." That, Jim failed to understand. "The choice was a moral one, therefore—if I didn't let up on you, Jamie would continue to suffer." That, Jim did understand.

Jim was not against going for couples therapy. He had no quarrel with a female therapist. (His mind had leaped to his deceased mother when Celia proposed it, rearousing in his stomach that hollow feeling he had experienced so many times in his youth when his mother exerted that mysterious power she seemed to have over both him and his father.) He had no opinion of Anne, positive or negative.

The idea of couples therapy exhausted, rather than repelled him. Swept by an all too familiar feeling of confusion, he thought again of his father. In part, his bond with Dad was reactive—a secret pact, a conspiracy against Mom. But why secret? Why, as Jim had wished so many times, had Dad never challenged her openly? She was not a demon, and in no way was she a tyrant. No, her power was from a kind of pervasive presence, just one huge eye, seeing all (was that the source of his fear of Celia's "cynical eye"?). Coming away from an encounter with Mom always left Jim confused, as if she were more in control of his own reality than he himself was. After such encounters, he felt impelled to seek out his father, seeking the comforting psychological embrace that both restored his sense of reality and swore him to conspiratorial silence. But then why did his father never say something? Why did his father never do anything?

Trying unsuccessfully at first to push down the anger that he rarely allowed himself, Jim felt his heart tear in two. To let anger in was to be disloyal. "Let gratefulness prevail," he had always concluded, "and loyalty—to both." With this reminder, his anger dissolved.

Now he thought of Celia and the pull-out couch, symbol of their sexual impasse. Anger reentered, with confusion and exhaustion. At whom was he angry? Celia, for one. For her power over him, which he conveniently brushed out of his consciousness most of the time. Wasn't his pleasure in the anticipation of John's battle with her a dead giveaway? His father, for another. Wasn't his secret alliance with John another dead giveaway? Whereas he and his father would not challenge women, John seemed to enjoy the battle of the sexes. Jim pictured John thriving on his victories, even sexual victories. "Not a pretty picture," he said, almost loud enough for Celia to hear, as he settled in finally to start his letter to his father.

CHANGE—AS REPORTED ON THE THERAPIST'S PINK (TERMINATION) FORM

The Pink Form has 22 items. John's responses on 14 of these are especially revealing.

Item #1. Client's view:
On the attached list of presenting problems, circle one or more items, ordering their importance in the therapy by numbering "1," "2," "3," etc., if more than one was presented. *[John's response]* "school problem," 2, and "other—being depressed and having night terrors" 1.

Item #2. Your view at termination:
Briefly describe in systemic terms the problem you dealt with. *[John's response]* The identified

patient, Jamie (aged 8), was caught up in a triangle owing to an unaddressed marital struggle.

Item #4. Were your therapeutic goals reached? That is, was the problem resolved or the symptom relieved? (Check one.)
  (a) Yes _____, No _____, Yes/No X
  (b) Comment: Jamie's symptoms cleared, without ever being dealt with directly. With the couple, there was some improvement in communication, but their problems were not completely resolved.

Item #5. Were the client(s)' individual goals reached?
  (a) *List names of family members, indicating "yes" or "no" for each.*
    Jamie — yes
    Rachael — yes
    Andrea — yes
    Celia — no
    Jim — yes
  (b) *In any case, please comment: [John's response]* Jim wanted Jamie's problem solved, but didn't seem to savor couples work. Celia would have wanted couples work in the beginning. [*Note:* It seems that John is still understating his induction into the couple system difficulties.]

Item #6. How does the family structure at termination compare with your system map and design for change at the outset?
[John's response] At the outset, both Celia and Jim had Jamie tied up in covert coalitions against the other parent. At termination, each parent had legitimate alliances with the son, which were out in the open and more or less supported by the other parent. The result was the elimination of Jamie's symptoms.

Item # 7. Termination was initiated by:
  ( ) a) client (specify)
  (X) b) therapist
  ( ) c) mutual agreement
  ( ) d) insurance ran out
  ( ) e) other
  In the margin, John scribbled the following: "It would be more accurate to say 'we.' Right, Anne? Right, David?" This addendum was dated 3 weeks after the date John completed the form. Presumably, it was inspired by a supervi-

sion session with Anne *and* the forms. Messages like this, usually to David, are common. Often, they are testy; occasionally, they are insulting. They represent a wish to believe that what therapists say really counts, that they and their form products really *are* "in the loop."

Item #8. Given your treatment method (your clinical approach in this case), did therapy end as expected?
- (a) Yes X, No _____, Yes/No _____, Don't know _____.
- (b) In any case, please comment:
  [John's response] According to my "method," therapy should have taken 15 sessions. It took 22. Pretty much on schedule, considering. . . .

Item # 9. Were you in any way surprised?
- (a) Yes X, No _____.
- (b) *Please comment: [John's response]* In part. Until Anne (as my case management supervisor) along with the forms (Satan take them!) reminded me, I wasn't paying attention to the length of therapy. *[Note:* This is not quite accurate—see next item.]

Item #10. Describe the termination sequence as best you can (reviewing back forms if necessary).
- (a) Don't know how _____, It's clear X, It's not clear but I'll try _____, Effort is a bother _____ (check one only)
- (b) *Description: [John's response]*
  1) I was going along pretty much on target and had planned on doing a little work with the couple system.
  2) Mrs. H. missed a session. I *was* surprised. *[Note:* He might have added, " . . . and annoyed, but ignored the import of her act or my reaction."]
  3) In her absence, I shifted focus to Mr. H. and the kids.
  4) Anne helped me discover that I was unfocused. *[Note:* More, that the therapy was "drifting."]
  5) Mrs. H. returned, missing a session here and there. *[Note:* John is smoothing off the rough edges of the rockiest part of the therapy.]
  6) I ended the therapy. *[Note:* John is putting himself more in charge than he actually was. More accurately, John and Celia ended the therapy. The boundary profile feature activated in the case is still operating.]

Item #12. What if anything did you (i.e., your

boundary profile) contribute to the way in which therapy ended?*
- (a) Nothing _____, Some X, Much _____.
- (b) *Explain: [John's response]* I may have been involved in a "forming structure" which I was not sufficiently on top of. I am working on this in private. *[Note:* John is still choosing to exercise strict boundary controls by keeping his boundary profile data out of the public domain.]

Item #13. What did your model (as distinct from your method) contribute to the way therapy ended?
- (a) Don't know _____, Do know _____, Don't know, but X.
- (b) *Explain: [John's response]* I know that it did. But to tell the truth, I don't know enough about my model yet. I am now getting a glimpse of the fact that, as Kantor insists, I may have one. *[Note:* Actually, Kantor would say "that one is beginning to evolve." He would also say that "John is on schedule; that he should discover the status of his model in his next and final year of training."]

Item # 14. What did the client(s) contribute?
- (a) Do know _____, Don't know _____, Don't know but X.
- (b) *Explain: [John's response]* Anne is of the opinion that the "status of sexual politics" both in the family and in the couple system may have had a great deal to do not only with the *ending* of therapy but with all of it. I confess that I did not pay a lot of attention to those politics. I concentrated on the couple *as parents* and on how the workings of the parental system affected the kids, especially Jamie, the identified patient.

In focusing on the couple as parents, John was in line with the guidelines of his brief strategic method. It is not clear that Anne took so strong a view on the matter as John suggests, but certainly, "sexual politics" was central to Celia's view of the problem, the therapy, and the termination. Anne, who was sensitive to this view, would be confusing John if she imposed it. She would then be failing to make the distinction between John's method and her model, which does tend to focus on the couple, couple sexual politics, and couples therapy, even when a child is presented as the problem.

Item #15. Did you modify your method as a result of your work with this family?

(a) No _____, Yes _____, Don't know X.

(b) *Explain: [John's response]* I think so. Something happened, during the therapy I did, without "knowing" what, or why. From my work with the H's I learned something important about the relationship between "couple" issues and "parenting" issues. I guess I should build what I learned into my method . . . sometime. But I am not prepared yet to modify the method, which worked pretty well.

To his credit, John has a mind of his own. It may be that the direction his model is taking will not match that of his present supervisor. As a trainer, Anne is responsible for knowing when to impose constraints on her supervisee's clinical perceptions and activities and when to encourage autonomy.

Item #17. Indicate (by a check) your rating of this therapy's success/failure.

( ) very successful
(X) moderately successful
( ) neither here nor there
( ) moderately unsuccessful
( ) very unsuccessful

Answers to questions like this one are "subjective," but needed. When therapists have access to their clients' responses to similar questions (as we intend at The Family Center), we will be moving assessment of outcome in a promising direction.

Item # 21. About seeing them again if they should return, would you:

(a) be eager _____, be reluctant X, be indifferent _____, advise against _____, refuse _____.

(b) *Please explain what is involved in your response: [John's response]* I think I muffed it with Mrs. Halpern and maybe with Mr. Halpern, too.

CONCLUSION

In this case approach, outcome is conceptualized as the reflection of a complex set of interactions and co-influencing events and relationships. In essence, it often contains varied and, at times, differing perspectives on the therapy experience. For example, Jim and Celia tended to agree on the beneficial effects of therapy for the children, but they differed in their feelings about the overall experience with the therapy and its effect on their marital relationship. If outcome studies stopped at the parental level, this case could have been classified as totally successful. When the Halpern family's views on therapy (especially on the marital level) are included in the assessment, however, the perspective on outcome shifts to reflect mixed reviews.

Furthermore, once the therapist, the supervisor, the therapist-supervisor relationship, and the uses of the research itself are included in the therapy-outcome feedback loop, the perspective on the overall therapy process changes again. Other influences and different vantage points emerge as elements that contribute both to therapy and to outcome evaluation. Instead of regarding John's "near impasse" in therapy and his redefinition of the family treatment unit as simply a manifestation of a difference between his chosen method (treatment plan) and actual in-session interventions, these phenomena can be studied more cybernetically for what they reveal in context. The underlying patterns that help create these occurrences can be studied as mismatches between (1) therapist's method and therapist's model, (2) the therapist's model and the family's model of reality, and (3) the mutual reciprocal effects of family on therapist and therapist on family.

The discrepancies often noted between what a therapist sets out to do and what actually happens session by session can, at times, be a function of misapplied technique (when a therapist-trainee needs to know more about formal methods), or it may reflect appropriate reappraisals on the part of the therapist. In other instances, these in-therapy changes in method result from the operation of boundary profile issues, forming structures, and an underlying conflict between the therapist's and the client's models of reality. These questions need to be systematically studied if therapists and researchers are to understand the multiplicity of influences that create outcomes.

REFERENCE

Kantor, D., & Andreozzi, L.L. (1985). The cybernetics of family therapy and family therapy research. In J.C. Hansen (Ed.), Family therapy collection: vol. 15. Integrating research and clinical practice. Rockville, MD: Aspen Systems Corporation.

6

The Medical versus the Educational Model as a Base for Family Therapy Research

Bernard G. Guerney, Jr., Ph.D.
Professor of Human Development
Head, Individual and Family
    Consultation Center
The Pennsylvania State University
University Park, Pennsylvania

ALMOST EVERYTHING THE family therapist says has an effect, positive or negative, on the progress the family will make. Sometimes a mistake can be crucial: what the therapist says or does not say and what the therapist does or does not do may cause the family to terminate therapy. In any hour of family therapy, therefore, the therapist must make scores of decisions. Generally, a therapist feels alone in making these decisions. The office may not be oval-shaped, but for the therapist, the buck stops right there just the same. At least the President has advisors. Having completed training, to whom can the family therapist turn?

There should be someone to help the therapist with the decision making, and that someone should be the family therapy researcher. The proper role of family therapy researchers, whose arena, after all, is that of applied research, is to provide family therapists with the type of knowledge they need to make each methodological choice and each verbal and nonverbal interaction with families more helpful.

Unfortunately, the family therapist has so far received little help from the researcher. Why do the journals have so many articles suggesting methods the family therapist might use, so many articles discussing the adequacy or inadequacy of current research methods in the study of family therapy, and so very few articles reporting the kind of hard research evidence that therapists need to make better daily therapeutic decisions? Doubtless, there are many reasons, and therapists themselves may be partly to blame. Perhaps they are too willing to pay attention to theorists or therapists who make their pitches without any data, too willing to pay serious attention to anecdotal reports and to case studies. Perhaps therapists must learn to be more demanding before those who have ideas and techniques to sell will feel obliged to support their presentations with data.

There may be a deeper reason for the lack of an appropriate climate for down-to-earth, practical research, however. It is that both the practitioner and the theorist/teacher/researcher are unknowingly trapped in a conceptual iron mask that restricts their freedom to demand or to conduct bigger, bolder, better, and more practical research. That iron mask is the medical model. The major theories, methods, and techniques of family therapy and, therefore, the major part of the research effort in family therapy follow the medical model and suffer from the conceptual restrictions it imposes. The alternative to the medical model, the educational model, promises a freer, more productive research effort (Guerney, 1977; Guerney, Guerney, & Stollak, 1971/72; Guerney, Stollak, & Guerney, 1970, 1971).

While the medical model is an appropriate model for treating disorders that are predominantly physical or biochemical in nature (including schizophrenia, severe depression, and the like), by methods which change the individual's biochemistry, it is not the best model for helping those whose problems are predominantly psychosocial in nature. For helping distressed families, it is almost ludicrously inappropriate. Although the medical model held a virtual monopoly in the realm of individual psychotherapy until the last decade or two and still holds a near monopoly in the realm of family therapy, the reasons for its supremacy in psychotherapy and family therapy are historical, social, and economic, and not a matter of relative efficacy (Authier, Gustafson, Guerney, & Kasdorf, 1975; Guerney, 1982).

It is important to realize that any type of family therapy that does not involve manipulation of clients by the therapist can be converted into the educational model of delivering services. It's not a question of what is taught, but whether or not the key concepts are systematically taught to the clients. The issue is whether the clients use the skills to solve their problems themselves or the therapist uses the skills to bring about the changes the therapist sees as desirable.

Much confusion stems from the use of the term *therapy* for the process of helping family members to overcome problems. One of the reasons that it has been so difficult to overthrow the medical model conceptually and practically is that it established the terminology used to describe the helping process. It would be preferable to replace the term *family therapy* with a term such as *family enhancement*, which would encompass families that wish to improve themselves, whether they are typical or atypical, happy or unhappy, harmonious or conflicted, functioning well or functioning poorly. Likewise, it would be much better to replace the term *family therapist* with a term such as *family consultant*. (The term *family educator* has already been claimed by a different type of professional.) As is the case with language changes in general, however, it will probably be easier to keep the same terminology, but drop the conceptual base (medical) that originally gave rise to the term.

Diagrammatically, each of the five steps in the medical and educational paradigms of family therapy may be compared as follows:

MEDICAL: 1. Pathology → 2. diagnosis → 3. prescription → 4. treatment → 5. problem removal/cure

EDUCATIONAL: 1. Ambition → 2. value clarification and goal setting → 3. program selection → 4. programmatic instruction → 5. knowledge, skill acquisition/goal attainment.

Implicit within these conceptual differences is a host of other differences in attitude and behaviors that affect the ways in which family therapy research can be conducted.

PATHOLOGY VERSUS AMBITION

The medical model focuses on family pathology. Therapists who operate within this model focus primarily on what is abnormal, atypical, and dysfunctional in the family; they try to eliminate disorders. The family in therapy is viewed as requiring not just a degree of help, but a type of help different from that which would benefit other families. Therapists with this view are often willing to treat families whom they label "pathological" in ways that they would not allow their own families to be treated by any professional (e.g., "paradoxical" instruction). Furthermore, because they believe that they are encouraging behavior that is "well" rather than "sick," they feel that they have the right to make a host of decisions on the family's behalf as to what are appropriate ways for family members to interact, instead of having the family members decide such matters themselves.

From the perspective of the educational model, a therapist's preference in a client's behavior or a family's interaction derives not from physical realities, as determined by a medical condition, but from the therapist's own particular value system, as determined by the sociocultural background of the therapist or by the sociocultural background of the therapist's favorite theorist. Although the therapist who follows the educational model may have opinions about the way in which family members should behave, the therapist sees his or her preferred behavior not in terms of pathology/wellness, but as a value choice that the family is free to accept or reject. The therapist sees families as having their own psychosocial and relationship goals, that is, as having ambitions. (With involuntary clients, it is sometimes necessary first to establish which of their goals are being frustrated by their antisocial behavior and which are being frustrated by those societal forces that have dominion over their future.)

Whereas the therapist following the medical model seeks to identify the pathology in the family, the therapist following the educational model seeks to identify the psychosocial ambitions and goals of the family. The focus is not on eliminating weaknesses, but on building the strengths necessary for the family to achieve those goals. The family members do not discuss what is wrong, but what they want; the therapist does not discuss what the family members are doing wrong, but teaches them what they need to know and how they need to behave to get what they want. The problems are eliminated along with the achievement of the positive goals. A major research advantage stems from this difference—the opportunity to gain statistical power, which derives from the greater ease of recruiting subjects when an educational model is followed.

The greatest single technical deficiency of family therapy studies is that the number of subjects involved is frequently too small to ensure an adequate test of the questions or hypotheses being investigated. Studies with negative results are often published when the chances of a type II error—a conclusion that no difference exists when one actually does—are enormously high because of the small number of subjects per experimental condition. Not only are such studies published, but even worse, reviewers and summarizers of research regularly include such studies in their reviews; worst of all, reviewers regularly give these studies a weight equal to that of studies with positive results. In literature reviews, therefore, one frequently encounters statements of this nature: "Jones found that X therapy was effective. However, the evidence is mixed: Smith did not find X therapy to be effective." Apparently, many research reviewers are unfamiliar with the basic scientific dictum that "the absence of evidence is not the same as evidence of absence." If Smith used a different type of subject, less qualified therapists, or less sensitive measures, or studied fewer subjects than did Jones (one or more of which is almost always the case), Smith's results do not in the least call Jones' results into question or make the effectiveness of therapy X equivocal. This being the case, it is especially important that researchers employ adequate numbers of subjects, lest practicing therapists be led astray.

The use of the medical model to determine what types of families are "eligible" for family therapy studies creates unnecessary problems in recruiting subjects. A view of families that seek therapy as qualitatively different from other families closes the door on subjects who do not qualify as "sick." In a medical model view of the nature of therapy, it is inappropriate to use therapeutic techniques with families that are not certifiably pathological, but merely want help in accomplishing positive family goals. In a view of therapy as a teaching, helping process, however, families that simply want to achieve better relationships need not be excluded from studies; indeed, they should be invited to participate. From the perspective of the educational model, helping families to achieve their desired psychosocial changes between and within family members is the essence of therapy. The basic process of therapy is no different whether the family is typical or atypical, in deep distress or in no distress, but merely wanting things to be better than they are.

It is true, of course, that families with differing degrees or types of motivation, or with differing levels of stress may vary in the length of time required to change or in the degree of change following therapy. Furthermore, such a pattern may differ according to the method of therapy used; for example, highly distressed families may, generally speaking, respond much better to therapy A than to therapy B. There is no reason to assume in advance, however, that the type of family pathology (e.g., enmeshment, anorexism, alcoholism) or the degree of family pathology is an appropriate dimension to employ in choosing or in describing a study sample. It may be found that these variables are much less important in assessing the impact of a given method of therapy or in comparing one type of therapy to another than other variables that are not diagnostic in nature (e.g., demographic variables, average intelligence of the family, fluency in the language of the therapist, emotional expressiveness, use of humor, or the extent to which rewards and/or punishments are used).

To decide, in the absence of evidence, that the level or type of pathology should determine the type of sample appropriate in studying the effectiveness of a therapeutic method is to make it unnecessarily difficult to recruit an adequate sample and, hence, to diminish the statistical power of the study. Early studies of a therapeutic method, especially— and what school of family therapy is not in the early stages of assessment?— should use diversified samples. Studies with targeted, range-restricted samples should come later, following clinical and data-based leads obtained with diversified samples. Early research should not rest on medical model preconceptions about the type or the degree of influence that ''pathology'' may have on the results or on the generalizability of results.

DIAGNOSIS VERSUS VALUE CLARIFICATION AND GOAL SETTING

In the medical model, it is the first task of the family therapist to determine precisely what has led to the dysfunction. For example, is the family triangulated, enmeshed, or disengaged? This concern with the genesis and nature of problems is necessary within the medical model because therapy focuses on fixing what is wrong. In the educational model, however, the therapist focuses on helping the family to define its goals: how family members would like to be able to treat others in the family and be treated by them, and what their group and individual psychosocial ambitions are. The therapist then teaches family members what they need to know to accomplish those ambitions. Because accomplishing those positives removes the antecedent negatives, there is no need for the family therapist to identify those negatives or to operate on them directly. For example, training each member of a triangulated family to express disagreement directly and openly to all other family members, and to treat each other's communications with respect and compassion eliminates the triangulation without a consideration of the triangulation or its causes per se.

The research implications of this difference in perspective overlap considerably with those already discussed, but two additional research advantages develop from this particular difference between the two models: a greater disposition to use random assignment to treatment and the use of analog studies. With a view of family therapy as a way to help families achieve their goals, without concern about diagnosing problems, researchers are much more likely to feel free to employ random assignment to treatment conditions rather than feel obligated to match groups on the basis of the diagnostic category into which they fall. The attempt to match subjects in different treatment conditions often leads to their being mismatched on variables that the investigator never considered. Given large samples (which we have already pointed out can be more readily obtained with an educational model orientation) random assignment to treatments is a much better research procedure. The greater the uncertainty that the matching variable is truly important or that it can be validly measured, the greater the advantage in using random assignment. Much uncertainty remains about the importance and validity of diagnostic decisions made by family therapists. Thus, nonconcern about diagnosis of families that characterizes the educational model encourages the researcher to make the better research choice.

Researchers who accept the educational model also would have a greater willingness to make carefully controlled analog studies a part of their armamentarium. If neither level nor type of disorder is assumed without evidence to be of crucial importance in assessing the effectiveness of the methods and techniques that family therapists use to bring about change in families, analog studies will be recognized as extremely useful. Analog studies are conducted with subjects who are not seeking help, but have been recruited simply as research subjects. Actual families, for example, may either role-play problems determined by the investigator or work on problems experienced by the family as a whole or by one of its members. (All families, it may be presumed, have some problems, whether or not they are of the type that would drive them to seek professional help.) A therapeutic method or technique is the independent variable. Process variables (e.g., feelings and behaviors generated by the method or technique) or outcome variables (e.g., the family members' satisfaction with solutions to problems) are the dependent variables.

Although the results of analog studies cannot be generalized to actual therapy with full confidence, such studies would help to determine what therapeutic techniques are likely to lead to what sorts of feelings and actions among family members and to establish a firm basis for clinical decision making. Families coming not for help but as subjects in a study could be selected and compared more easily for a host of characteristics other than pathological characteristics (e.g., intelligence or age of youngest member). All sorts of techniques could be employed with a consistency that would be impractical or ethically questionable with families that are seeking help. The effects of interactions among techniques (e.g., self-disclosure, joining, interpretations, humor, metaphors) or the effects of various sequences and timing patterns among such techniques could be studied in ways not possible in actual therapy. Not only techniques, but also methods of therapy (e.g., structural versus strategic) similarly could be studied in much more controlled ways. More precise and complete data, including physiological responses to particular types of interventions, if desired, could be secured.

Such research seems likely to provide a much firmer base for daily therapeutic decision making than do less well controlled studies that have as their main feature only that the clients had severe problems and were seen in a professional context. Almost all other applied fields depend heavily on the use of such "laboratory" or analog studies. The medical model restricts the use of such studies in the field of family therapy, however, by its principle that entirely unique circumstances are created by pathology. If, on the other hand, therapy is conceptualized as "an intervention" and the variables of interest are seen as the emotions, interpersonal reactions, and behaviors generated by various types of interventions, it is not unreasonable to assume that studying the reactions of families recruited for research purposes will shed light on the reactions of families seeking help.

PRESCRIPTIONS AND TREATMENTS VERSUS PROGRAM SELECTION AND TEACHING

In the medical model, each therapy meeting is likely to be viewed as a unique challenge. The therapist tries, moment to moment, to catch or to create therapeutic opportunities out of the spontaneous, fluid, shifting interactions of the family members. The therapist enters each session with a prescription for what needs to be done, based on the diagnosis (e.g., too enmeshed, too disengaged, power misalignment) to change the family interaction patterns in the appropriate way and a plan to apply special techniques (e.g., home assignments, paradoxical instruction) to remove the difficulty.

In contrast, after determining the goals of the family, the therapist who follows an educational model selects one or more programmatic instructional systems (e.g., rational-emotive, grief management, relationship enhancement, value clarification, or assertiveness) to use in teaching family members what they need to know to achieve their goals. The therapist approaches each session with a teaching agenda of the particular subskills that the family members will be taught in the session (e.g., empathic

responding, expressive skill, usages of self-statements, or positive reinforcement in changing behavior). Using a standard set of teaching skills and procedures (e.g., demonstration, modeling, verbal and nonverbal reinforcement) and standard materials (e.g., readings, audiotapes, homework logs, videotapes), the therapist teaches these subskills. The problems, if any, that the family members work on are determined not only by their concerns, but also by the skills that they are "scheduled" to acquire or practice during the session. The therapist controls the family interaction process in order to accomplish the teaching agenda and does not rely on the family's spontaneous, moment-to-moment statements and interactions for inspiration.

In terms of research, the major advantage of programmatic instruction is the replicability of the treatment process. The teaching methods used in educational model of therapy are far more easily taught to therapists and far easier to repeat across families and across family problems than are the types of interventions used in the traditional, predominant types of family therapy.

Replicability is the sine qua non of any research. Yet, much family therapy "research" seems to be conducted without great visible concern about replicability. Without replicability, however, the research may be of value only to the therapist who did the study, not to other therapists in the field. The less the capacity for accurate repetition of a study by many therapists, the less reliable the information gained about a therapeutic method or about the differential effects of different methods. The more clearly a particular family therapy method is defined in terms of how therapists should deal with any particular set of circumstances that arise during the therapeutic hour, the more a therapist can rely on research on that method to make appropriate therapeutic decisions.

Educational model treatment approaches are, by the nature of their assumptions and mode of attack, much more clearly defined and much more replicable than are those based on a medical model. Therefore, the advantages of the educational model for research, especially for the kind useful to the decision-making therapist, are enormous.

PROBLEM REMOVAL VERSUS ACQUISITION OF KNOWLEDGE/ SKILLS

In the medical model, family therapy is considered fully successful if the family has been restored to an average, "normal" level. The concept of cure is essentially a subtractive process that is oriented toward the past: the problems that the family had earlier have been removed. In the educational model of family therapy, the concept of success is an additive one that is oriented toward the future: the family has acquired the skills necessary to solve not only the problems for which it sought help, but also the psychosocial problems that may arise in the future. The family has a greater capacity, because of the knowledge and skills acquired, than has the average family to make psychosocial choices, to resolve family problems and conflicts, to attain family goals, and also to help one another resolve individual psychosocial problems and attain individual psychosocial goals.

From the perspective of the educational model, the distinctions among family problem prevention, family enrichment, and family therapy are quantitative, reflecting the point at which the training experience is undertaken, the length of time it requires, and the frequency with which certain types of difficulties are likely to be encountered. These three areas of intervention are not regarded as qualitatively different with respect to either processes or objectives. Thus, generalization to a wide range of issues, circumstances, and settings, and the goal of instilling lifelong skills are inherent parts of the educational model of family therapy.

The educational model of family therapy expands the outcome criteria of research. Instead of measuring outcome only in terms of the removal of symptoms or the elimination of negative patterns, as is done under the medical model, the educational model prompts the therapist to add positives to the assessment (e.g., feelings of love, harmony, and happiness). At outcome, the normal versus abnormal perspective of the medical model leads the therapist to think only in terms of normative measurement (standardized, normed tests). The goal achievement orientation of the educational model, while allowing for the use of normative measures, encourages the therapist to consider also the use of ipsative measurement, such as goal attainment scaling.

Generalization of what has been learned in therapy to situations outside the family is another outcome variable more likely to be considered in assessing educational model therapies than medical model therapies. The knowledge and skills taught in educational model therapies are often applicable in non-family settings (e.g., with co-workers and friends). It seems likely that generalization reflects the strength and durability of what has been learned in the therapy per se.

CONCLUSION

The major difference between the medical model and the educational model of family therapy is that therapists who follow the medical model use their skills to solve a family's problems, while those who follow the educational model teach the family members those aspects of therapeutic skills that the family members need to solve present and future problems themselves. If more researchers recognize the value of the concepts underlying the educational model of family therapy, some significant gains in the type of family therapy research most useful to practicing family therapists may be expected.

REFERENCES

Authier, J., Gustafson, K., Guerney, B.G., Jr., & Kasdorf, J.A. (1975). The psychological practitioner as a teacher: A theoretical-historical practical review. *The Counseling Psychologist, 5*(2), 31–50.

Guerney, B.G., Jr. (1977). Should teachers treat illiteracy, hypocalligraphy and dysmathematica? *Canadian Counselor, 12*(1), 9–14.

Guerney, B.G., Jr. (1982). The delivery of mental health services: Spiritual vs. medical vs. educational models. In T.R. Vallance & R.M. Sabre (Eds.), *Mental health services in transition: A policy sourcebook* (pp. 239–256). New York: Human Sciences Press.

Guerney, B.G., Jr., Guerney, L., & Stollak, G. (1971/72). The potential advantages of changing from a medical to an educational model in practicing psychology. *Interpersonal Development, 2*(4), 238–245.

Guerney, B.G., Jr., Stollak, G.E., & Guerney, L. (1970). A format for a new mode of psychological practice: Or, how to escape a zombie. *The Counseling Psychologist, 2*(2), 97–104.

Guerney, B.G., Jr., Stollak, G., & Guerney, L. (1971). The practicing psychologist as educator—An alternative to the medical practitioner model. *Professional Psychology, 2*(3), 276–282.

7

Dyadic Interaction Patterns

Robert A. Ravich, M.D.
New York, New York

F AMILY THERAPISTS GENER- ally agree that their field came into existence in the mid-1950s. At almost exactly the same time, the introduction of neuroleptic drugs, notably chlorpromazine hydrochloride (Thorazine), led to increasingly intensive efforts among neuroscientists to understand the modes of action of tranquilizers and antidepressants. While these two therapeutic approaches—marital/family therapy and neuropharmacology—appear to be in sharp contrast to one another, they involve very similar shifts in the focus of attention. While therapists were shifting their attention from individuals to relationships, neuroscientists were shifting theirs from the neuron to the synapse. Marital/family therapists have focused so intensely on variations in their therapeutic interventions that they have largely failed to recognize their own involvement in an aspect of the neurosciences that has important clinical applications.

FROM NEURON TO SYNAPSE

The basic unit of the brain was long believed to be the neuron, or nerve cell. Although the human brain is made up of several million neurons, the connections between them, known as synapses, are far more numerous; several billion synapses are known to exist. With the development of neuroleptic and antidepressant drugs during the past two decades, increased attention is being directed to these synapses. There has been mounting evidence that these psychoactive drugs affect the release and uptake of neurotransmitters, a group of natural chemical substances that carry messages between one neuron and another across a space known as the synaptic cleft or the synaptic gap. Synapses in higher organisms have been found to be virtually indissoluble conjointures. Thus, when methods were developed for extracting synapses from minced brains, the synapses remained intact as units. They were contained within a vesicle, or bubble, and these were called synaptosomes. The dynamic behavior of synapses is inferred by combining neurochemical, neuropharmacological, and neurophysiological knowledge with structural knowledge about synaptosomes (Jones, D.G., 1975).

FROM INDIVIDUAL TO RELATIONSHIP

Is psychiatric research on the family needed? Is it timely? Is it feasible? My answer is an emphatic "yes" to these questions. The need to formulate the dynamics of the family group as a psychological entity in and of itself, *to search out means for classifying family types* according to their mode of adaptation and mental health . . . represents an urgent priority.

This is especially conspicuous in disordered marital relationships. . . . In the clinical study of family relationships one can frequently discern a subtle shift in the location of the pathogenic focus of anxiety and conflict. At one point, the greatest weight of pathogenic disturbance will be contained within the personality of a particular member. It may then shift and become expressed predominantly as conflict *in the zone between this person and another family member*. (Ackerman, 1957, emphasis added)

The origins of the concept of between go back to Buber's famous essay *I and Thou* (1937). In 1957, Buber further explored the distinction he had repeatedly made between the "social" and the "interhuman":

By the sphere of the interhuman I mean solely actual happenings between men, whether wholly mutual or tending to grow into mutual relations. For the participation of both partners is in principle indispensable. The sphere of the interhuman is one in which a person is confronted by the other. . . . It is basically erroneous to try to understand the interhuman phenomena as psychological. When two men converse together, the psychological is certainly an important part of the situation, as each listens and each prepares to speak. Yet this is only the hidden accompaniment to the conversation itself, the phonetic event fraught with meaning, whose meaning is to be found neither in one of the two partners, nor in both together, but only in their dialogue itself, in this "between" which they live together.

Buber's concept of the sphere of between can affect the way that a therapist actually works with couples. The therapist who always looks at the person who is speaking, for example, may not see that the other person is giving out signals by facial expression, body language, and posture that are just as important as what is being said. Although maintaining a center of focus on a point somewhere between the couple causes the therapist to miss all nonverbal communications, it has an advantage. Within a very few moments, it evokes questions as to which person should talk. If the therapist sits quietly or shrugs, the couple resolves this and begins.

Each couple seems to bring a "game" into the room at every session. The game is essentially the same each time, even though the subject matter covered during each session may be very different. The opening moves of a game are relatively simple, compared with the much more complex and subtle rules that determine the continuation of the game. The couples may not "know" their own rule system, even though they obey it absolutely and at all times.

EXPERIMENTAL GAMES

Two game models were being used experimentally by social psychologists in the mid-1960s. The more widely used was known as the Prisoner's Dilemma (Rapoport & Chammah, 1965). It was by far the simpler of the two; but because the decision making in the task was to be done with neither verbal nor nonverbal communication, it was inappropriate for married couples. It was more concerned with the decisions made than with the process of decision making.

The other game model, the Acme-Bolt Trucking Game, was developed by Deutsch, who was interested primarily in conflict and conflict resolution. He created the game after seeing two trucks on a narrow road with their front ends facing each other and no room to pass; the drivers were out of the cabs gesticulating wildly, each attempting to convince the other to back up and allow his own truck to pass through the narrow section first. While the Trucking Game was more complex technically, it did measure and record the process of interaction (Deutsch, 1973; Deutsch & Krauss, 1960, 1962).

A study of 30 couples who played the Trucking Game showed that a great deal could be learned from their discussions about the ways in which they had played the game. Their discussions indicated very clearly, and usually quite spontaneously, that the Trucking Game revealed many of the rules and metarules that intimate dyads used repeatedly (Ravich 1966, 1969; Ravich, Deutsch, & Brown, 1966). It was so successful that it was adapted for use in the clinic setting, appearing as the three-dimensional Train Game (Jones, S., 1968).

RAVICH INTERPERSONAL GAME-TEST (RIG/T)

The apparatus for the Ravich Interpersonal Game-Test (RIG/T) is a 3 foot by 4 foot table with a 14-inch shoulder-high screen running down the middle. When seated in the chairs on opposite sides of the table, subjects can see the other's face, but not what he or she is doing on the table behind the screen.

On each side of the screen there are identical electric trains on identical tracks, along with control panels for operating the trains. The players are instructed to move their train engine from a starting point to a finishing point; they may choose a direct route, which is very short, or an alternate route, which is long. Pennies are awarded to the players for each second under 30 seconds that it takes them to reach the goal; pennies are taken away for each second over 30 seconds. The use of the direct track may produce a gain; the use of the alternate track always leads to a loss, however, since it takes the engine approximately 45 seconds to reach the goal by this route.

Each player has a control that allows him or her to place an electric barrier across the other person's direct route. Even if neither uses the barrier, both will be stopped if their trains are at identical points on the same section of the direct route at the same time, referred to as a collision. When this occurs, either or both players may back up or stand still. If one person backs up, the other person can move forward and proceed on the direct route. At any time, a player may return to the start and switch to the other route. There are neither barriers nor collisions on the alternate route.

Players are free to talk with each other during the test. The tester instructs the players only in the operation of the equipment. There are no instructions given regarding the couple's choices or behavior. Because the tester does not preclude any actions that the couple may want to take, the test is totally projective in nature.

The game is played over 20 trials or "trips." A complete test takes 45 to 50 minutes. The first 10 trips are considered trials. The basic dyadic interaction pattern is assessed on the basis of trips 11 through 18.

Clinical Material

Two types of information are collected and stored while a couple is participating in the RIG/T. Data on the decisions made individually and jointly by the two players and the actions taken on their control panels are electronically collected on each trip. In addition, the game is recorded on videotape with the use of two cameras and a special effects generator that provides a split-screen image of the two players as they sit and play the RIG/T.

The control panel data are used to create a graph that shows it as a "final common pathway" in an interacting system of intimate dyads. Nine distinct patterns of interaction have been identified, and all can be recognized in sequences of four trips. The patterns are visually clear, and the clinician can quickly become familiar with their characteristics and their diagnostic meaning, prognosis, and therapeutic indications, much as a cardiologist learns to "read" an electrocardiogram. These are graphs of strategies, not numbers. The two lines represent the tactics of each player. Their positions on the graph, the amplitudes of change, and the relationship between the lines are the significant factors.

The three graphs in Figure 1 depict interactions in which both players use the direct route on each trip and neither closes the other's barrier. In this cooperative pattern, the players alternate finishing first on each trip in the sequence. In the dominant-submissive pattern, player ☐ finishes first on each trip. The cooperative, dominant-submissive pattern combines features of the first two. Some players may start on either the direct or the alternate routes, but are likely to change from one to the other, especially from direct to alternate (Figure 2); they may also make use of the barriers. In general, interactions of these types lead to losses for one or both players on all or most trips. This differs from the patterns in Figure 1, in which both players are likely to have profits or only small losses. There are exceptions to this when prolonged collisions occur, however.

The interaction patterns in Figure 3 all involve the use of the alternate route, which avoids the possibility of colliding or of being blocked by the other player's barrier. Losses are inevitable in these patterns; they are limited, however, since they cannot be affected by the other player. In cooperative avoidance, one player takes the direct route, the other takes the alternate route, and they trade the routes taken on each successive trip. This pattern has been termed the "marriage-divorce paradox" (Ravich, 1972). The competitive pattern is a special kind of interaction that is analogous to trench warfare. Both players close their barriers and take the alternate route. In game theory, this is known as the "mini-max solution" (Ravich & Wyden, 1974). Mutual avoidance in which both players simply take the alternate route is a not uncommon phenomenon on the first trip or on a single trip somewhere in the course of a complete test. When it occurs

Figure 1 Patterns of Interaction in the RIG/T When Both Players Use the Direct Route

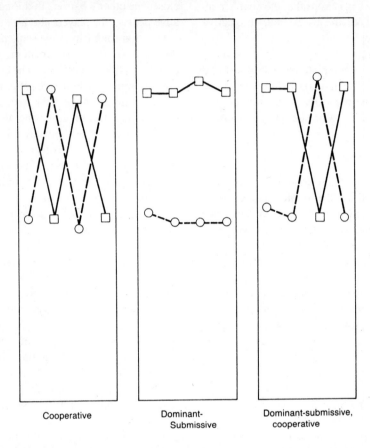

Cooperative   Dominant-   Dominant-submissive,
                               Submissive   cooperative

more often, it reflects an extreme degree of nonrelatedness.

Perla (1985) has shown that Hogan was responsible for combining videotape recording with the RIG/T. He played back these recordings in post-game sessions, showing the couple their behavior on the split screen. In this way he successfully demonstrated directly to the couple their patterns of interactions and their intricate verbal messages and body language. He believed that this combination of RIG/T and video made richer interpretation in marital therapy possible and

allowed more progress to be made in the treatment of distressed couples. Hogan employed this combination of RIG/T and videotape with almost 100 couples during a five-year period (Hogan, 1975).

The coordinated interactions of the hands on the control panel have provided the clearest evidence of a dyadic synapse that links the two members of an intimate pair. In every couple I have tested, highly synchronized interactive behaviors have occurred at extremely rapid rates during one or more segments lasting several seconds to almost 30 sec-

Figure 2 Interaction Patterns in the RIG/T When Players Change Routes

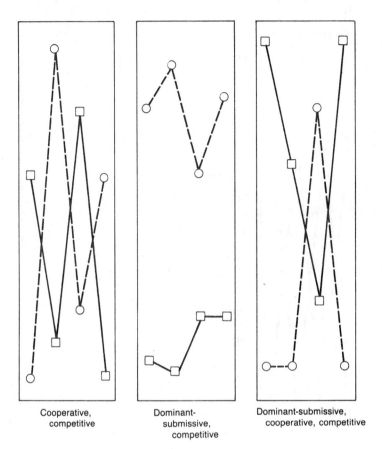

| Cooperative, competitive | Dominant-submissive, competitive | Dominant-submissive, cooperative, competitive |

onds. The significance of these bursts of interaction is heightened by the fact that the players cannot see the other's hands at all while playing the game. The split-screen arrangement of the camera images allows this phenomenon to be observed clearly, although it is often necessary to view the film one frame at a time to appreciate this interactive behavior.

Clinical Examples

Research studies carried out by Liebowitz & Black (1974), Edelman (1980), and Perla (1985), using factor analytic approaches on groups of dyads, have identified two important factor loadings. According to Perla (1985), "the first factor loads heavily on all those outcome measures other than collisions; and the second factor loads heavily on the three measures directly relating to collisions." She refers to the first factor as "covert competition" and the second factor as "overt competition."

Stan and Linda Lake had very few collisions, used their barriers to block each other on the direct route,

Figure 3 Patterns of Interaction in the RIG/T When Both Players Use the Alternate
Route

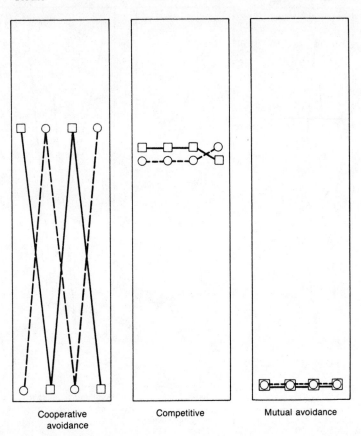

Cooperative
avoidance

Competitive

Mutual avoidance

started out on the alternate route often, or changed from the direct to the alternate route when they saw that they had been blocked by the other's barrier. John and Blanche Wren played a very different game. After the second trip, they both took the direct route every time, and neither used the barrier. Inevitably, they had many collisions. The Lakes lost much more than did the Wrens, however, because they forced each other to take the alternate route by

their almost unremitting use of the barriers. The game played by the Lakes essentially showed a dominant-submissive, competitive pattern, while the Wrens' pattern was essentially cooperative or cooperative, dominant-submissive.

The prognosis for the continuation of these marriages is guarded, but for entirely different reasons. The Lakes are too inclined to block each other, thereby maintaining a distance between them. In the sense that they do not confront each other, their competition is "covert." The Wrens, on the other hand, confront each other all the time; they are repeatedly bumping into each other, constantly irritating one another.

In couples with serious marital disorders, therapists must determine whether individual or conjoint therapy is indicated and what the specific goals of therapy should be. The couple's type of interaction can have a significant bearing on both these decisions. A prognostically hopeful event occurred quite late in the course of the games played by the Lakes and the Wrens.

On their 14th trip, Stan and Linda Lake both took the direct route and remained on it. They had a collision lasting 2 seconds, and they did not close their barriers. On the 17th trip, they again took the direct route, had two collisions lasting 15 seconds, and only Stan closed his barrier for a very short time (4 seconds). Although they returned to their competitive manner of play on the next trips, these trips indicated to them and to their therapists that there was some possibility of spontaneous, constructive change on which therapy might be based. Subsequent therapy has tended to confirm this, although there did not appear to be any such possibility originally.

After the 18th trip, the Lakes were told that they could not use the alternate routes. This had a profound effect. They became locked in collisions 23 times, lasting a total of 120 seconds on the 19th trip. This behavior suggests that the serious difficulty

in resolving conflict when they are on the same path is the basis of their almost constant distancing.

The Wrens, who always took the direct route and, after the second trip, never closed their barriers, became locked in recurrent and mounting cycles of collisions. On the 5th trip, they had 18 collisions, lasting 28 seconds; on the 10th trip, there were 12 collisions, lasting 39 seconds; and on the 14th trip, they had 34 collisions, lasting 73 seconds. Suddenly and unexpectedly, they began to work together effectively, avoided collisions entirely, and began to play cooperatively. Couples that encounter the degree of frustration experienced by the Wrens are more likely to become increasingly competitive, closing the barriers on one another. The prognostically hopeful sign in this case is the fact that they could achieve this degree of cooperation. The problem that needs to be addressed in therapy is why it takes so very long to appear.

CONCLUSION

Cromwell, Olson, and Fournier (1976) and Klier (1978) have raised objections to the Train Game on the grounds that it is an "observational method with low task relevancy." They contrast this general type of methodology with self-reports of conflict and with observational methods in which couples interact concerning real life marital issues. It is precisely the "low task relevancy" of the RIG/T and its videotaping by means of the split-screen technique within a focused laboratory setting that have made it possible to recognize the synaptic quality of interaction of intimate dyads, however. Ackerman (1957) realized "the rudiments of a useful science of social psychology" that could make it possible "to search out means for classifying family types." He could also "discern a subtle shift in the location of the . . . focus of anxiety and conflict [from] within the personality of a particular

member [to] the zone between this person and another member." The research of Deutsch, applied to the study of marital dyads, has led to the formulation of a typology based on patterns of interaction in the videotaped RIG/T situation. This is a means of operationalizing and recording the complex sphere of between defined by Buber.

REFERENCES

Ackerman, N.W. (1957). An orientation to psychiatric research on the family. *Journal of Marriage and the Family, 19*, 68–74.

Buber, M. (1937). *I and thou* (R.G. Smith, Trans.). Edinburgh: R. & R. Clark.

Buber, M. (1957). Elements of the interhuman. *Psychiatry: Journal for the Study of Interpersonal Processes, 20*, 105–113.

Cromwell, R.E., Olson, D.H.L., & Fournier, D.J. (1976). Tools and techniques for diagnosis in marital and family therapy. *Family Process, 15*, 1–49.

Deutsch, M. (1973). *The resolution of conflict: constructive and destructive processes*. New Haven, CT: Yale University Press.

Deutsch, M., & Krauss, R.M. (1960). The effect of threat upon interpersonal bargaining. *Journal of Abnormal and Social Psychology, 61*, 181–189.

Deutsch, M., & Krauss, R.M. (1962). Studies of interpersonal bargaining. *Journal of Conflict Resolution, 6*, 52–76.

Edelman, P.D. (1980). *The Ravich Interpersonal Game-Test: A factor analytic study and comparison with the Bales' SYMLOG space*. Unpublished second year graduate project, Harvard University, Boston.

Hogan, P. (1975). Creativity in the family. In F.F. Flach (Ed.), *Creative Psychiatry*. Geigy, 1975. West Caldwell, N.J.: CIBA-Geigy.

Jones, D.G. (1975). *Synapses and synaptosomes: Morphological aspects*. New York: Wiley.

Jones, S. (1968, December 28). Game is set to get collision-bound marriages on track. *New York Times, 41*.

Klier, J. (1978). *Comparison of verbal behaviors and outcome constructiveness between high-adjustment and low-adjustment couples during conflict resolution*. Unpublished doctoral dissertation, Rutgers University, New Brunswick, NJ.

Liebowitz, B., & Black, M. (1974). The structure of the Ravich Interpersonal Game-Test (RIG/T). *Family Process, 13*, 169–183.

Perla, C. (1985). Internality-externality and interpersonal trust as predictors of cooperative behavior among married couples in the Ravich Interpersonal Game-Test. Unpublished doctoral dissertation, Florida Institute of Technology, Melbourne, Florida.

Rapoport, A., & Chammah, A.M. (1965). *Prisoner's Dilemma*. Ann Arbor, MI: University of Michigan Press.

Ravich, R.A. (1966). Short-term intensive treatment of marital discord. *Voices, 2*, 42–48.

Ravich, R.A. (1969). The use of an interpersonal game-test in conjoint marital psychotherapy. *American Journal of Psychotherapy, 23*, 217–229.

Ravich, R.A. (1972). The marriage/divorce paradox. In C. Sager & H.S. Kaplan (Eds.), *Progress in group and family therapy*. New York: Brunner/Mazel.

Ravich, R.A., Deutsch, M., & Brown, B. (1966). An experimental study of marital discord and decision making. In I.M. Cohen (Ed.), *Family Structure, dynamics and therapy* (pp. 91–94).

Psychiatric Research Report No. 20. Washington, DC: American Psychiatric Association.

Ravich, R.A., & Wyden, B. (1974). *Predictable pairing*. New York: Wyden.

8

The Conflict between the Ethics of Therapy and Outcome Research in Family Therapy

Anthony P. Jurich, Ph.D.
Kansas State University
Manhattan, Kansas

Candyce S. Russell, Ph.D.
Kansas State University
Manhattan, Kansas

E THICS IS A WORD THAT brings to mind "human rights," "fair play," and "solutions to conflicting interests," issues that have always been crucial in both the creation and the utilization of the social sciences. Social science researchers have long struggled with the issue of ethics in the collection, analysis, and dissemination of their data (Abramson, 1977; Barnes, 1963; Klockars & O'Connor, 1979; LaRossa, Bennett, & Gelles, 1981; Reynolds, 1979; Wolfensburger, 1967). Similarly, most social science practitioners have created a code of ethics to regulate the practice of their profession (e.g., American Association for Marriage and Family Therapy, 1982; American Association of Sex Educators, Counselors, and Therapists, 1980; American Psychological Association, 1977). The priority of ethics in the field of marriage and family therapy is reflected in the fact that the first volume of the *Family Therapy Collections* was devoted to an examination of ethics (L'Abate, 1982).

It is in the area of evaluation research that these two sets of ethics are drawn together. Although these two ethical traditions are very similar, there are significant areas of difference. In most cases, the ethics of therapy are more restrictive than are the ethics of research. Few professionals have written about the effects of the more restrictive ethics of therapy on evaluation research, however. Guttentag and Struening (1975), for example, discussed the ethics of evaluation research, but they focused on the questionable motivations for and the misuse of the results. Because of the unique ethical standards with which therapists are faced, the evaluation of any type of therapy poses a particular set of problems for the researcher.

In the study of family therapy, the evaluation of therapy is especially complex. There are multiple reports from members of the same family, and information at the level of the whole system is inaccessible, making research of family therapy a difficult job (LaRossa et al., 1981). There are more barriers to overcome in evaluation research of family therapy, therefore, than in evaluation research of individual therapy. In order to guide the researcher, several authors have outlined procedures for conducting evaluation research of family therapy with minimal flaws in research design (Gurman & Kniskern, 1978, 1981; Joanning, 1984; Wells & Dezen, 1978). Ethical considerations generic to the profession of family therapy may be in direct conflict with some of these procedures, however.

DESIGN ISSUES

One of the greatest challenges to evaluation research in family therapy centers on the use of a control group. Research design, especially when subjects are not randomly selected, mandates the use of control groups (Gurman & Kniskern, 1981; Joanning, 1984). Ideally, the family therapy researcher establishes a treatment group (a group to be treated by means of the therapeutic technique being tested), an alternative treatment group (a group to be treated by means of a therapeutic technique that is in some way different from the technique being tested), and a nontreatment control group (a group not to be treated at all). This design meets several challenges to exter-

nal and internal validity, but it also poses several ethical problems.

In most cases, a therapist-researcher chooses to do evaluation research because he or she believes that a specific mode of therapy or therapeutic technique is better than other methods for treating a given problem. As a researcher, he or she wants to explore such therapeutic hunches, and the least ambiguous way to do so is to use control groups. As a therapist, however, the practitioner finds that this research design requires him or her to recommend to a client an alternative treatment that is suspected of being an inferior treatment. Such a recommendation is not consistent with the therapist's ethical commitment to provide the *best* possible therapy for the client.

It is even more questionable to assign a client family to a nontreatment control group. Because withholding therapy poses such an ethical problem, most researchers use families on their waiting list as their nontreatment control group (Gurman & Kniskern, 1981). They ask clients to wait from 1 to 6 weeks before receiving treatment. This also poses an ethical dilemma, however, since the problems in some families may grow worse without appropriate treatment. Gurman & Kniskern (1981) suggested that a solution to this ethical problem is to employ a method called "treatment on demand" (DiMascio & Klerman, 1977), in which the client family is asked to wait, but is given the option of coming into therapy when they feel it necessary. Although such therapy on demand would be limited in number or length of sessions, this approach may solve some of the problems surrounding a nontreatment control group; even so, it does not eliminate the basic ethical consideration of withholding treatment from a potentially needy client family.

The assignment of client families to different control groups creates an additional ethical problem. Under strict experimental design techniques, this assignment should be random. For example, the first client family seeking treatment should be assigned to the treatment group; the second, to the alternative treatment group; and the third, to the nontreatment group. This method is fine, if the families are faceless numbers in a statistical formula. However, what if the first family has a mild problem, caused by a developmental transitional dilemma, while the second family has a problem that is known to be especially responsive to the therapy being tested? What if the third family has a suicidal family member? Can the therapist ethically justify a random assignment strategy when he or she strongly suspects that the therapy received as a result of the assignment will not be the best therapy for that family or will even be harmful or dangerous to the family? In these cases, the therapeutic imperatives outweigh the considerations of optimum research designs.

Differences in therapists may further complicate the situation. For example, one therapist may have difficulty with a specific type of case. If the research design dictates the random assignment of that therapist to this very type of case, can the therapist-researcher ethically make the assignment? This problem can be overcome by having only one therapist do the therapy for each treatment group, but the effect of the therapy is then contaminated by a potential therapist effect. In other words, the study may not test the effectiveness of the therapy modalities, but the effectiveness of the individual therapists. Such a design has a serious flaw. Furthermore, this type of specialization is not possible in most clinic settings. Therefore, the ethical dilemma again arises as to whether to assign cases based on statistical randomization as dictated by the rigors of research or based on the ethical imperatives dictated by the pledge to give client families the best treatment possible. In most cases, therapeutic ethics win out, and the design of the study suffers.

The degree of structure that the research design imposes on treatment is also a problem in clinical research. In most experimental designs, the treatment is held constant across cases (Campbell & Stanley, 1963). Few clinicians, however, consider their therapy a "constant." The nature of therapy is dynamic; the therapist reacts to the family's input and responds accordingly. There is no predetermined protocol for therapy. A research design that restricts the structure or process of therapy may fulfill the requirements of research, but may result in inferior therapy for the client family and may be a poor test of therapy as it is actually practiced. Process research, which allows for intervention variations, presents fewer ethical problems than does a predefined treatment package. As the elements of process in therapy increase, however, interpretation of the data becomes more complex.

THE ASSESSMENT BATTERY

Several factors must be considered in deciding on the type of assessment that will be used during possible pretest, post-test, and follow-up periods (Gurman & Kniskern, 1981). Should the family be asked to trudge through a battery of pencil-and-paper tests? If such an assessment procedure is used, how long should it be? Who should take these tests? Researchers are often tempted to construct a battery of sophisticated, multidimensional scales from which they can glean multiple patterns of family interaction, each family member's personality, and a detailed description of the family environment. When faced with such a battery, however, family members may be tempted to drop out of therapy. The sheer length of the instrument battery can be overwhelming to the family, especially to a family under stress. Does the therapist-researcher have an ethical right to escalate the stress of the client family under these conditions?

Even if the size of the assessment instruments is manageable, the family may have some problems in completing them. Clients who read poorly may perceive the pencil-and-paper instruments as a "put-down," denigrating them for their lack of reading skill. Stroke patients may be literally unable to fill out the forms. If the family's executive system is faulty, the pencil-and-paper test may accent an unclear hierarchy or further decrease the status of an illiterate adult in the family's hierarchy. If one parent has markedly more education or a higher level of intelligence than does the other parent, the assessment instrument may accentuate the power differential, further devaluing one parent in front of the children and escalating conflict without the therapist's ever being fully aware of the volatile nature of the situation. Because the therapist may have no idea of the effect of the pretherapy assessment procedure on the family, either as indi-

viduals or as a whole system, the assessment battery itself becomes an intervention with unplanned and unanticipated results.

Many researchers seek to obtain data on family interaction through unobtrusive observation (Humphreys, 1970; LaRossa et al., 1981). Direct observation makes it possible to obtain information that the family may be reluctant to discuss or may not even know. The principle of informed consent requires the therapist to inform family members that they are being observed, however, and that very act of informing may prompt them to alter their behavior, thus creating a reactive situation in which the observation is no longer unobtrusive.

Not only because of the research ethic of informed consent, but also because of the therapeutic need to build trust and client rapport, the therapist-researcher must be open and honest in explaining his or her research design. Home visits to interview and observe the family are relatively open, but they may contaminate the research, since the visit itself is a form of intervention (LaRossa et al., 1981). Even in a strict observation, the family is placed in a different set of circumstances. Either the researcher is a guest in the family's home, or the family is asked to congregate in a therapy room. For the family seeking therapy, either of these can be considered some form of therapeutic intervention.

The timing of data collection, particularly the pretherapy assessment, leads the researcher into another ethical dilemma. Families that go to a clinic for help expect to be assigned a therapist who, in some way, will aid them. They do not expect to walk into the office and take a battery of tests, to "play a family game" at a computer terminal, or to be told to wait in a room and be themselves (while they are observed by a researcher). Surely, they are at least confused by a process that they do not understand. Yet, if the process is explained to them, the very act of explanation will contaminate the assessment. Furthermore, after they complete the assessment, the family members may not be informed of the results. After spending anywhere from one-half hour to three hours completing an assessment, nobody tells them what it means. If they should inquire as to the results, they may be told that the assessment instrument is very sophisticated and, in some cases, must be sent away for a computerized report that will not arrive for 2 to 3 weeks (Ryder, in press). These procedures may interfere with or at least prolong the joining process in therapy. Furthermore, these so-called unobtrusive procedures violate the principle of informed consent.

UNIT OF ANALYSIS

Family therapy outcome research is unique in that the unit of analysis is not a "given" and frequently involves more than one subsystem. A researcher may wish to collect information on the individual, on a variety of dyadic relationships (e.g. marital, parent-child, sibling), and/or on a larger system (e.g., nuclear family, binuclear family, or extended kin group).

In most research, the investigator is able to assure the research participant of complete confidentiality, extending to family members. When dyadic relationships or the family system as a whole is the unit of analysis and the assessment procedure involves observation of inter-action, however, family members reveal information to one another as well as to the researcher. For instance, when a family is asked to discuss plans for launching their teen-ager into adulthood (e.g., Riskin, 1982), a new level of openness may be required, and information may be revealed that might not otherwise be overtly divulged (e.g., the parents' disagreement over the appropriate age for leaving home or information about Dad's launching from his family of orientation). A therapist may argue that revealing such family "secrets" is therapeutic, but a family member who has agreed to participate in the research procedure may not fully understand the extent of the information that may be revealed. This issue is most problematic for families that have been assigned to a control group and will not necessarily follow the collection of interactional data and where family "secrets" have been exposed.

There are several subsystems potentially involved in family therapy, and it is quite common for the therapeutic focus to shift from one subsystem to another throughout the course of therapy. For example, a family may focus initially on a child (e.g., for a substance abuse issue), move to marital therapy, and finally seek divorce counseling. Over the course of that family's therapy, sessions may be held for the nuclear family group, the adolescent alone, the marital couple conjointly and separately, and possibly even each spouse with his or her parents. Furthermore, the subsystems participating in the therapy for one family that must deal with adolescent substance abuse may be different from the subsystems participating in the therapy of another family that has the same symptom. Thus, the researcher ends up with different treatments across subjects as well as information from varying family subsystems. In short, the researcher's unit of analysis can become quite unclear.

If the nuclear family is taken as the unit of analysis, the researcher can anticipate that at least some family members will be unwilling to participate in therapy. If the marital dyad is selected as the unit of analysis, the researcher can anticipate that at least some couples will have a child who is experiencing a crisis and will require some joint family sessions. To withhold conjoint family sessions would be unethical, just as it might be unwise to urge reluctant family members to participate in order to meet the requirements of the research protocol (Hines & Hare-Mustin, 1978).

CONCLUSION

The intent of this chapter is not to discourage clinical research in family therapy, nor is it intended to excuse poorly designed, inadequately monitored research. Clearly, the evaluation of family therapy outcome carries with it special limitations. These limitations should be taken into account not only by researchers who design outcome studies, but also by clinicians who are consumers of such research:

1. Research designs used in family therapy are likely to indicate whether treatment B is better than treatment A or better than treatment B given "on demand" in response to mounting stress. They will not determine whether treatments A and B are better than no treatment at all so long as the client families are from a true clinic population and, therefore, at

least moderately distressed. Nevertheless, the results of such research are very helpful to the practitioner who must choose among treatment A, treatment B, or treatment B "on demand." Withholding all treatment is not a viable option for the practitioner, just as it is not an ethical option for the researcher.

2. The primary contract with clients is for therapy, not for research. The collection of data postpones traditional treatment, may escalate stress levels within the family, and sometimes discourages joining with the therapist. Therefore, researchers must be selective about the information they collect, and some questions must go unanswered.

3. Extensive pretesting, in itself, may be a form of treatment. In the absence of large sample sizes, of random assignment to treatment conditions, and of post-test only research designs conducted concurrently with both pretest and post-test designs (e.g., Solomon Four Design as described by Campbell and Stanley [1963]), the impact of pretesting cannot be separated from the impact of therapy. If pretesting is minimally time-consuming and is easily administered, however, the pretesting can be considered part of the subsequent treatment package. This lays the groundwork for clinicians to continue to collect data and participate in the research process.

4. Subject families are dropped from analyses at a higher rate than are subjects from studies of individual therapy since families will agree to release information only to the degree that the least comfortable family

member agrees. These families may be more "resistant" to therapy or simply slower to make a commitment to outsiders than are those families who agree to pretesting as well as to research participation. The anecdotal reports of therapists with regard to the "treatability" of these families and the pace at which they "join" with outsiders would be useful in determining whether the data that have been fully collected and analyzed may be biased.

Because it is essential to respect clients' rights, researchers will finish with an incomplete picture of the therapy process and with some questions unanswered. However, practitioners may be able to operate, and in fact improve on their therapy, without answering such "ultimate" questions.

REFERENCES

Abramson, P.R. (1977). Ethical requirements for research on human sexual behavior: From the perspective of participating subjects. *Journal of Social Issues, 33,* 184–192.

American Association for Marriage and Family Therapy. (1982). *Ethical principles for family therapists.* Washington, DC: American Association for Marriage and Family Therapy.

American Association of Sex Educators, Counselors and Therapists. (1980). *AASECT code of ethics.* Washington, DC: American Association of Sex Educators, Counselors and Therapists.

American Psychological Association. (1977). *Standards for providers of psychological services.* Washington, DC: American Psychological Association.

Barnes, J.A. (1963). Some ethical problems in modern fieldwork. *British Journal of Sociology, 14,* 118–134.

Campbell, D.T., & Stanley, J.C. (1963). *Experimental and quasi-experimental designs for research.* Chicago: Rand McNally.

DiMascio, A., & Klerman, G. (1977, June). *An appropriate control group for psychotherapy research in depression.* Paper presented at the Society for Psychotherapy Research, Madison, WI.

Gurman, A.S., & Kniskern, D.P. (1978). Research on marriage and family therapy: Progress, perspective, and prospect. In S.L. Garfield & A.E. Bergin (Eds.), *Handbook of psychotherapy and behavior change* (2nd ed.). New York: Wiley.

Gurman, A.S., & Kniskern, D.P. (1981). Family therapy outcome research: Knowns and unknowns. In A.S. Gurman & D.P. Kniskern (Eds.), *Handbook of family therapy* (pp. 742–775). New York: Brunner/Mazel.

Guttentag, M., & Struening, E.L. (1975). *Handbook of evaluation research* (Vols. 1 and 2). Beverly Hills, CA: Sage.

Hines, P.M., & Hare-Mustin, R.T. (1978). Ethical concerns in family therapy. *Professional Psychology, 9,* 165–171.

Humphreys, L. (1970). *Tearoom trade: Impersonal sex in public places.* Chicago: Aldine.

Joanning, H. (1984). *Major design features and considerations for outcome research in family therapy.* Unpublished manuscript.

Klockars, C.B., & O'Connor, F.W. (1979). *Deviance and decency: The ethics of research with human subjects.* Beverly Hills, CA: Sage.

L'Abate, L. (Ed.). (1982). *Values, ethics, legalities and the family therapist.* Rockville, MD: Aspen Systems Corporation.

LaRossa, R., Bennett, L.A., & Gelles, R.J. (1981). Ethical dilemmas in qualitative family research. *Journal of Marriage and the Family, 43,* 303–313.

Reynolds, P.D. (1979). *Ethical dilemmas and social science research.* San Francisco: Jossey-Bass.

Riskin, J. (1982). Research on "nonlabeled" families: A longitudinal study (pp. 45–66). In F.

Walsh (Ed.), *Normal family processes*. New York: Guilford Press.

Ryder, R.G. (in press). Professionals' values in assessment. *Journal of Counseling and Values*.

Wells, R.A., & Dezen, A.E. (1978). The results of family therapy revisited: The nonverbal methods. *Family Process, 17,* 251–274.

Wolfensburger, W. (1967). Ethical issues in research with human subjects. *Science, 155,* 47–51.

Family Therapy Practice and Research: A Dialogue

Bradford P. Keeney, Ph.D.
Texas Tech University
Lubbock, Texas

James P. Morris, M.S.
Texas Tech University
Lubbock, Texas

Therapist: What does science prove?

Researcher: Science proves nothing. Unfortunately, when a researcher's (or therapist's) hypothesis seems to be on target, we sometimes make the mistake of speaking of "confirmation" and believing that we've trapped a piece of solid reality.

Therapist: Do you mean that science will never be able to prove that family therapy works? I thought the verdict had already been reached and that it was for family therapy.

Researcher: Science can never prove anything.

Therapist: I'm confused about what scientific research can do for me. Let's start again by defining *science*.

Researcher: I'm not sure that I can help with the confusion, but I can provide a definition. Science prescribes a systematic way of knowing about the relation of irreducible and stubborn facts to abstract general principles.

Therapist: That sounds like Alfred North Whitehead.

Researcher: You're right. By "general principles" I mean tautologically designed symbolic systems, often referred to as formal theory, while "irreducible and stubborn facts" refers more to the domain of empirical observation. On the one hand, for example, you could have Euclidean geometry; on the other hand, you could have your measurements. Scientific investigation simply explores the relation between these two levels of knowing.

Therapist: The critical points for me concern the definitions of *empirical observations* and *theoretical principles.* As a therapist who follows the ideas of cybernetics and systems theory, I know that I never have immediate access to raw data. As an observer, I actively participate in the construction of my observations.

Researcher: In other words, there is no such thing as theory-free observation. As Popper [1959] once proposed, our discoveries are guided by theory, rather than theories being discovered through observation.

Therapist: That's it. My theories help construct the phenomena that they are designed to explain. Hanson [1958] said it somewhat differently: "A theory is a cluster of conclusions in search of a premise" [p. 157].

Researcher: With this view, the clinician as well as the researcher can be seen as an active constructor of therapeutic and research realities. Explanation has to do with the ways that therapists and researchers use particular theoretical or epistemological recipes to describe the construction of their observations. Such a view might enable us to see the practice of therapy and the conduct of research as more similar than different.

Therapist: Again, we find that science has nothing to do with proof of observations. Instead, it has to do with the invention of new theoretical principles that lead to new experiential realities.

Researcher: Remember that we're talking about a cybernetic view of science. Other scientists and therapists may view science through a different epistemological lens.

Therapist: Before proceeding, let's define what we mean by cybernetics.

Researcher: Cybernetics is a tradition of scholarship that is generally concerned with the science of discerning and managing patterns of organization, whether these patterns organize neuronal events, conversations, social systems, or family therapy. Keeney [1983] set forth the application of cybernetic ideas to family therapy in his book *Aesthetics of Change.*

Therapist: Given the framework of cybernetics, what does it mean when we say "clinical research"?

Researcher: Research becomes a task of reexamining (i.e., re-searching) what one did to construct a particular therapeutic reality. Following Laing, we speak of "capta" rather than "data." We don't analyze data as representations of some objective state of events. Instead, we examine how our capta construct our experience. For instance, von Foerster suggested that we speak of perception as closer to an act of creation, as in conception, than to a passive state of affairs, as in reception.

Therapist: This more clearly explains why science can never prove anything. After all, all observations are self-verifying: they construct the phenomena that fit the theoretical system in which the observer believes.

Researcher: Research and therapy are also active probes—they invent and prescribe distinctions that lead to the construction of experiential realities.

Therapist: But how are research and therapy different?

Researcher: They are alike in that both set forth recipes for constructing experiential realities. They are different in the levels and kinds of realities that they construct. Family therapy research, for instance, is usually an experiential reality that is about the experiential reality of family therapy.

Therapist: One obvious point is that any claim for objectivity is nonsense. The absurdity of objectivity is illustrated by von Foerster (1976, p. 16). He said, "It is syntactically and semantically correct to say that subjective statements are made by subjects. Thus, correspondingly, we may say that objective statements are made by objects. It is only too bad these damned things don't make any statements."

Researcher: Most researchers would claim to agree that we can't really be objective. Unfortunately, because they go on using a representational rather than a constructivist view of data, their work remains deeply rooted to premises of objectivity, whether they fully realize it or not.

Therapist: In other words, they agree that their maps are not the territory, but they still assume that their maps are of some territory.

Researcher: Yes. The assumption that there really is some territory out there that can be mapped brings us back to the notions of objectivity. We then argue about how objective we are in examining a set of phenomena, although we may be willing to admit that complete objectivity is impossible to attain.

Therapist: Maybe what we're trying to say is that there is no territory.

Researcher: Or that the map *is* the territory. Stated differently, we have only maps of maps of maps, ad infinitum.

Therapist: And that is a cybernetic view: recursions within recursions.

Researcher: Let's assume that family therapists are interested in a cybernetic overhaul of research.

Therapist: Where would we begin?

Researcher: We might begin by saying that such an approach has already been demonstrated by the work of Bateson, the cybernetic pioneer of the social sciences. Bateson's view of research was vastly different from that of most American-educated social scientists.

Therapist: I would bet that many of these social scientists would even say that he didn't do any real research.

Researcher: Such a confession indicates the limitations of their own view of research.

Therapist: How did Bateson conduct his research?

Researcher: Weakland (1981) has given us a summary of the rules that governed the research conducted by Bateson and his colleagues on the paradox in human communication. For example, no one was to know what the project was about; there was a commitment to maintaining a dialectic between strict and loose thinking; the project was encouraged to roam all over the place; the researcher should focus on what is directly observable and question everything.

Therapist: That sounds like an interesting way to study family therapy, but is it really research? After all, I thought research had to do with carefully articulated hypotheses, operationalized variables, and statistical computations.

Researcher: You are referring to one recipe for constructing research. Bateson simply had another recipe. To claim that one recipe is the only correct and appropriate prescription for research is simply dishonest and unethical.

Therapist: I would like to hear you say that to the college professor who taught me experimental design in graduate school.

Researcher: Now we're talking about the politics of research. The family therapy and social science journals contain descriptions of an abundance of statistical techniques wedded to inductive thinking, objectivity, and quantitative analysis. Bateson, Lorenz, and Piaget, however, never published a $P<.05$ and sometimes boasted about not needing quantitative graphs to explain their ideas.

Therapist: Then there is a gap between the approaches of many of the giant pioneers of social science and what we're taught in graduate school about research.

Researcher: Science as a whole has been undergoing a major revolution. In addition, more and more scholars are recognizing that the major intellectual contributions of social science are seldom connected to what we have been taught about the so-called scientific method.

Therapist: Furthermore, researchers are becoming more and more aware of what we therapists have known, namely, that all research is part of a political context that dictates norms for theory and research. Graduate programs, postgraduate training programs, and editorial boards determine what theories and methodologies are to be mastered and, more importantly, which ones are to be ignored.

Researcher: The rules prescribing theory and research in family therapy and social science have been increasingly challenged for several decades. More and more scholars have stopped asking the question, "Is this or that science?" Instead, they ask, "What is science anyway, particularly with regard to understanding human experience?"

Therapist: It seems that the emerging view of science, as we've been talking about it, is a shift from a monological paradigm, in which the observer is not allowed to enter his or her descriptions, to a dialogical paradigm, in which descriptions reveal the nature of the observer. Gurman & Kniskern [1981] stated that "empirical research oriented toward discovery rather than verification is also in order" [p. 753].

Researcher: One distinction that is not always made clear when we talk about science is the difference between a context of discovery and invention, and a context of verification. Discovery and invention, the main business of science—not prediction or verification—has little to do with so-called experimental designs.

Therapist: I would certainly agree that what you do to discover and invent is a completely different activity from the strict procedures of classical experimental designs.

Researcher: Although some researchers are willing to acknowledge this difference, they are less willing to agree that there are different ways of arriving at formal verification. What is *news* to both therapists and researchers is that many strategies require different criteria of verification.

Therapist: Are you saying that there is really more to social science research than sociostatistical experimental designs?

Researcher: That's the big secret. In addition, we have to realize that improving experimental designs will yield little with respect to either discovery or further verification. For instance, if an absolutely perfect experimental design were executed, the so-called findings would still be entirely in the domain of interpretation. Any search for data that are free from human interpretation indicates a misunderstanding of human understanding.

Therapist: It seems a bit ironic that family therapy, which has boasted about being part of a new epistemology, is still largely connected to an old approach to social research.

Researcher: The epistemological revolution that transformed clinical practice and theory has yet to influence family therapy research. The next revolution in family therapy and social science will probably involve a cybernetic-systemic epistemology for the conduct of research. A new awakening should take place in our field in which practitioners and researchers will find themselves with a menu that offers many alternative research strategies.

Therapist: What are the names of these alternative approaches to social science research?

Researcher: They include ethology, ethnomethodology, cognitive anthropology, phenomenology, hermeneutics, frame analysis, cybernetics, sociolinguistics, and experimental epistemology, to name a few.

Therapist: Would you give me an example of how one of these alternative research strategies would be applied to the study of family therapy? Maybe you could comment on your own research.

Researcher: My own work concerns the development of cybernetic ethnographies of communication in the context of systemic therapy. Hymes [1974], one of the pioneers in ethnographical studies of communication, noted that it is a research method for directly investigating the use of language in particular contexts. He stated that it is a science that studies "communicative form and function in integral relation to each other" and that its "aim must be to keep the multiple hierarchy of relations among messages and contexts in view" [p. 5]. He added that very little work has been done in developing a cybernetic approach to ethnographic studies, although he acknowledged that two distinguished social scientists have made original contributions in developing such an approach—Levi-Strauss and Bateson.

Therapist: What is it you're trying to do?

Researcher: Most simply put, my colleagues and I are developing ways of observing systemic family therapy that will enable us to identify and articulate the most basic patterns that organize it. Since cybernetics is the science that is most concerned with developing a language for describing patterns, we utilize it as an epistemological base for orienting our work.

Therapist: Do you have any examples of this type of research?

Researcher: Several books have been written. One of these, *Mind in Therapy: Constructing Systemic Family Therapies* [Keeney & Ross, 1985], sets forth the basic patterns that organize the work of such systemic therapists as Haley, Weakland, Fishman, Silverstein, Boscolo, and Cecchin. Another book, *Systemic Therapy in Practice* [Keeney & Silverstein, in press], is a more detailed ethnographical study of a full case conducted by Olga Silverstein. All this work arises from a research context in which investigators have attempted to connect state-of-the-art ethnographical research methods with the finest examples of clinical work in the field.

Therapist: Are you comfortable working with traditional social scientists?

Researcher: Personally, I'm comfortable in a community of scholars that respects and encourages dialogue, including debate over the practice of classic experimental designs. What I find objectionable is any hierarchy that gives supremacy to sociostatistical experimental designs and relegates all other methodologies to second-class citizenship, or worse yet, to noncitizenship.

Therapist: Other methodologies too easily become disqualified as "descriptive research" that in due course may lead to the real thing, that is, operational and quantitative empirical research.

Researcher: That's the sort of thinking we have to correct.

Therapist: I remember being a doctoral student and wanting to "do research" on Whitaker's clinical work. I told my professor that I planned to observe videotapes of his work in order to figure out how to discover some basic patterns. I wish you'd been around at the time.

Researcher: I bet your professor looked at you as if you were crazy.

Therapist: Not only that, she kept insisting that I must operationalize variables, develop measurement techniques, and consider statistical analyses of my data. I told her that I wouldn't be able to discover what I was interested in if I did all that. She reminded me that there are rules for prescribing the conduct of research.

Researcher: You see, she failed to recognize that the most important part of your study was the question you posed for yourself. Your question or purpose of inquiry should determine the procedures that organize your research.

Therapist: But most family therapy researchers work the opposite way. Their experimental procedures determine what questions they are permitted to investigate.

Researcher: Perhaps the reason that many clinicians find a lot of family therapy research boring and noninformative has to do with the fact that many uninteresting questions are being asked.

Therapist: How did the field get into such a muddle?

Researcher: That's a good research question.

Therapist: But I couldn't answer it with a sociostatistical design. Let me ask you another question. What do you think will become of family therapy research?

Researcher: First of all, we can expect to hear more about the specific ways in which sociostatistical designs are often inappropriate for the study of social interaction and communication.

Therapist: Could we get a preview of some of these critiques?

Researcher: Most of these critiques are not new to social science, but may be new to the field of family therapy. For instance, Bakan [1966], in a classic article entitled "The Test of Significance in Psychological Research," argued that most experimental designs test the statistical null hypothesis in a context in which the experimenter has every reason to suppose that it is false.

Therapist: In other words, the experimenter isn't really experimenting—he is redundantly and trivially demonstrating what he already knows.

Researcher: Exactly. In addition, Bakan demonstrated that the majority of social scientists misunderstand and misuse statistical methods. From a different perspective of criticism, Bateson seriously doubted whether any events in human behavior could ever be counted so as to become members of a statistical sample.

Therapist: What about a batting average in baseball?

Researcher: Although such an average is indeed some sort of indication of better or worse, Bateson [1975] noted that two things must be considered.

First, "every play of the game is unique," and second, "every ball pitched is conceptually inseparable from others, forming with them a larger strategy" [p. 143].

Therapist: Thus, the most elementary requirement of statistics—uniformity of sample—is not even met in a baseball batting average.

Researcher: As Bateson [1975, p. 143] put it, "Into the same river no man can step twice; not because the universe is in flux, but because it is organized and integrated."

Therapist: As a therapist, my primary research interests concern learning how to see basic patterns that organize effective clinical work. Will statistics and quantitative research methods help me in this search?

Researcher: Quantity has little to do with identifying or explaining pattern. Even as far back as the 1940s, Kubie [1947, pp. 517–518] argued that "all quantitative formulations have at best only the limited value of descriptive shortcuts, and never provide a safe basis for explanations of behavior and of behavior differences."

Therapist: I remember reading a similar point in Bateson's [1979] book *Mind and Nature: A Necessary Unity*. But, again, why is it that traditional research methods are not appropriate for researching interactional patterns and social organization?

Researcher: McDermott and Roth [1978] of the Rockefeller University have argued that, when traditional methods of research are used to study social interaction, they seldom describe the behavior of the particular persons. Instead, "various biographical indices or facts about a person—gender, race, descendant line, occupation, and the like—are assumed to gloss adequately the person's relations with others, and the relations between the indices are taken as descriptions, often causally stated, of the social organization of the person's behavior" [p. 321].

Therapist: In other words, we're speaking of gross errors in logical typing. This would be like someone saying that he can use sociostatistical methods to study social interaction because it enables him to analyze the "statistical interaction of variables."

Researcher: That is an example of sheer nonsense.

Therapist: What else do you predict for the future of family therapy research?

Researcher: The future of family therapy research must include the recognition of alternative strategies of research—each with its own rules and ideas about discovery and verification.

Therapist: Family therapists will then not speak of *the* scientific method, but will speak of scientific methods or, even more generally, of a wide variety of formal methods of inquiry. Politically speaking, doctoral programs in family therapy and the social sciences must become more responsible and teach a wide variety of research approaches. This, in turn, would lead to more broadly educated clinicians, researchers, journal editors, and journal readers.

Researcher: This is already beginning to happen. For instance, I am part of a course in my university entitled "Alternative Strategies of Family Therapy Research."

Therapist: I wish my graduate education had provided opportunities to use research methods that would have been more responsive to the questions that captured my imagination.

Researcher: Let's not forget that sociostatistical methods sometimes do provide a useful service. People who are interested in using these methods might call themselves "clinical accountants." These professionals could conduct straightforward outcome assessments that would provide a consumer service for family therapy. The term *clinical accountant* not only more accurately acknowledges how sociostatistical methods may provide a service to family therapy, but also implicitly suggests that they are quite limited in responding to the more scientific questions.

Therapist: One thing we haven't mentioned is that the continued prominence of sociostatistical methods has a lot to do with the way in which people respond to authority. Most therapists think that all social science research is about experimental designs simply because they were told that by some authority figure in graduate school—a professor, journal editor, or textbook author.

Researcher: The problem of lineal authority goes beyond the homeostasis of family therapy research. It also seems to address the manner in which many therapists organize their own learning and clinical practice. How many therapists defend their work by saying, "Minuchin, or Bowen, or

Satir states that this is how you're *supposed* to work"?

Therapist: Do you think that the so-called authorities of family therapy learned how to practice by following such an authority?

Researcher: Of course not. They constructed a context of discovery in which their clients and their own unique clinical resources shaped a new strategy for practice. We might even want to call this context "research."

Therapist: One of the biggest problems with authority in the field of family therapy and social science concerns its obsession with scientism. I've never understood why social scientists feel so inferior to the hard sciences. They forget about "Heinz von Foerster's Theorem Number Two: The hard sciences are successful because they deal with the soft problems; the soft sciences are struggling because they deal with the hard problems" [von Foerster, 1981, p. 206]. Unfortunately, every year or so psychologists, psychiatrists, social workers, and family therapists nominate some scientist as their guru whose words are

some sort of magical incantation that will somehow lead to new clinical understandings and strategies.

Researcher: Some scientists from other disciplines have made fantastic contributions to family therapy, but we must challenge the way in which these scientists are used as authorities for disciplines in which they have no expertise. They may have quite a bit to teach us, but their teaching concerns the way in which they have addressed the problems of their context, level of observation, and phenomenal domain. It then becomes *our job* to construct our own approaches to the problems and contexts that confront us.

Therapist: Now you sound like a systemic therapist.

Researcher: That's a discovery! In conclusion, what do you finally propose as the major purpose of research in family therapy?

Therapist: It has something to do with inventing better questions.

Researcher: And what difference would that make?

Therapist: Let's find out.

REFERENCES

Bakan, D. (1966). The test of significance in psychological research. *Psychological Bulletin, 66,* 423–437.

Bateson, G. (1975). Some components of socialization for trance. *Ethos, 3,* 143–155.

Bateson, G. (1979). *Mind and nature: A necessary unity.* New York: Dutton.

Gurman, A., & Kniskern, D. (1981). Family therapy outcome research: Knowns and unknowns. In A. Gurman & D. Kniskern (Eds.), *Handbook of family therapy.* New York: Brunner/Mazel.

Hanson, N. (1958). *Patterns of discovery.* Cambridge, England: Cambridge University Press.

Hymes, D. (1974). *Foundations in sociolinguistics: An ethnographic approach.* Philadelphia: University of Pennsylvania Press.

Keeney, B. (1983). *Aesthetics of change.* New York: Guilford.

Keeney, B., & Ross, J. (1985). *Mind in therapy: Constructing systemic family therapies.* New York: Basic Books.

Keeney, B., & Silverstein, O. (in press). *Systemic therapy in practice.* New York: Guilford.

Kubie, L. (1947). The fallacious use of quantitative concepts in dynamic psychology. *Psychoanalytic Quarterly, 16,* 507–518.

McDermott, R., & Roth, D. (1978). The social organization of behavior: Interactional approaches. *Annual Review of Anthropology, 7,* 321–345.

Popper, K. (1959). *The logic of scientific discovery.* London: Hutchinson.

von Foerster, H. (1976). The need of perception for the perception of needs. In K. Wilson (Ed.), *The collected works of the biological computer laboratory.* Peoria, IL: Illinois Blueprint Corporation.

von Foerster, H. (1981). *Observing systems.* Seaside, CA: Intersystems Publications.

Weakland, J. (1981). One thing leads to another. In C. Wilder-Mott & J. Weakland (Eds.), *Rigor and imagination: Essays from the legacy of Gregory Bateson.* New York: Praeger.

Index